Education and Empowerment for the Twenty-First-Century Parent

A Practical Guide for Raising Healthy and Well-Adjusted Teens

Oppedisano/Cannon

2011

Contents

Chapter 1

Introduction

The American family has undergone dramatic changes over the course of the past sixty years. The family unit, once the most pivotal component of American culture, has steadily deteriorated. Previously considered a normal part of everyday life, sharing a meal as a family has become a rarity in many homes. The long-term consequence of this directly relates to the ability of parents to raise, protect, and guide their children through adolescence into adulthood. In an age when it often takes a combined income of two working parents to provide for their family, time must be recognized as a valued commodity. Scheduling family meals, outings, and recreation must become a priority. To develop and maintain strong bonds, parents and children must know each other well. Adolescents need to know that their parents can handle the diverse and complicated issues that affect them daily. If they fear that their parents cannot cope with the intensity of their problems, their willingness to express and discuss their issues will be greatly diminished.

Changes within the dominant American culture have also influenced the structure of the family unit. We live in a world with an increasingly laissez-faire attitude toward parenting. A detached parenting style can have dramatic and dire consequences. To be an actively engaged parent, there must be an understanding and awareness regarding the influences that affect a child development. The power of marketing and simple observation cannot be underestimated. Although we certainly agree that children should be allowed to express themselves and to have some leeway to make mistakes, there must be boundaries and limits in place that address maladaptive patterns of behavior. The setting of boundaries and limits is the responsibility of the parents, not society. This can be a very confusing and daunting role. This book will provide ways to set healthy boundaries and limits on risky, dangerous or even life-threatening behavior.

Unconditional love drives parents to protect their children at all costs. A thorough, tactical approach to parenting will help to empower families to limit their children exposure to risk. Though no one approach or method is fail proof, the reduction of risk and an increased knowledge base are critical. We need to be realistic and acknowledge that threats are constantly evolving. The images of the mass murder that took place at Columbine High School shattered the belief that schools are safe. Unfortunately, the fact that this is not the case has, since then, been repeatedly reinforced. Communication, trust, and strong familial bonds are at the core of a healthy, functional family. To focus on safety, parents and their children must strengthen their bonds and engage in open and honest dialogue.

The use of vignettes within this book will provide real-life anecdotes as cautionary tales. Parents, for instance, need to be aware of the common ploys that sex offenders use to lure their victims. From a safety standpoint, twenty-four-hour news networks have changed the way in which we, as Americans, view our country. Child abductions are often the lead story on many of the major news networks and provide the viewer with the horrors that a victimized family is experiencing. These stories have made our collective unconscious fearful of the predators hiding in the shadows. Unfortunately, these news pieces provide only a narrative without offering ways for parents to learn strategies and techniques to keep their families safe. To protect ourselves from predators, we must gain an understanding of their maladaptive and criminal behaviors. From the sex offender to the budding psychopath, behavioral indicators provide us with clear insight into ways to deter such horrific acts, as well as identify possible predators.

The study of human behavior is complex and intricate. As forensic psychologists, we have had the unique opportunity to interview and evaluate hundreds of convicted criminals housed in a variety of penal settings. Often, these criminals seem charming and likable. They have honed their craft as a way to take advantage of those who lack insight into their criminal plans. Manipulation and building superficial bonds are primary components of their skill set. This is often done by feigning or faking of empathy. Criminals are students of behavior. They are keenly aware that in order to establish trust with an unsuspecting victim, they must build and develop rapport. They need to seem likable, friendly, and, most important, trustworthy. By developing trust, their targets become more susceptible to victimization. This process takes time, commitment, and willingness by the perpetrator to be patient.

Intelligence gathering is a pivotal component of any assessment of risk. Parents need to familiarize themselves with the technology used by their children. If you are unaware of what is at your child's disposal, you will have no way to monitor and supervise. If you are not tech savvy, a simple solution may be to place the family computer in a common area within the house. Though this may not fit with your design aesthetic, it will give you the ability to monitor what sites are popping up on the computer screen. With the advancement of cell phone technology, parents need to consider seriously the type of phone that they want to provide for their child. Unrestricted access to the Internet has proven to be deadly in the case of many sex offenders who have found, befriended, and eventually targeted children whom they have met and manipulated online. Parents also need to be willing to snoop. We understand parent's desire to protect their child's privacy. In a world without threats, this may be a noble goal. Unfortunately, this is not conducive to current life in America. If you suspect that your child is using illicit drugs, carrying weapons, or communicating with an unknown person who may be dangerous, it is your responsibility as a parent to search backpacks, dresser drawers, and closets. To protect your children, you need to know where the risks lie.

Another extremely important point is that parents need to learn how to listen to their children. As a culture, we are so distracted by outside influences that our normal communication habits have been greatly altered. From text messages to e-mails, language has been reduced to acronyms and sentence fragments. Parents need to listen to the subtleties expressed by their children and teach them the importance of healthy dialogue. It is also critical to be aware of and understand the signs and symptoms of mental illness or mood disturbances so that you can differentiate between behaviors that are a normal part of adolescent development and those that are of greater concern. By developing a trusting relationship, parents will provide a safe environment in which children can talk openly. Furthermore, parents need to use appropriate and effective discipline strategies to reinforce good decision making and to establish clear rules and boundaries within the household.

Chapter 2

Parenting Questionnaire

We have compiled a list of questions to help stimulate thought and to establish a baseline for your parenting style. Use it as a guide to analyze your relationship with your children. Empowerment and education include a willingness to discover areas within your parenting toolbox that need improvement, or alternative strategies that help to foster behavioral change.

1. Did you have a healthy and interactive relationship with your own parents? Were you able to openly discuss issues with them? What type of discipline practices did they use?

2. How would you describe your current relationship with your children? Are they willing to discuss risky behaviors with you? Do you feel that the conversations are one-sided and lack depth or meaning? Do you feel like you preach and your suggestions fall on deaf ears?

3. How well do you know your kids? Are you aware of how many hours they spend online? How many social networking sites do they belong to?

4. What type of discipline strategy do you use within your household?

5. How would you rate your child's self-esteem? How does he/she respond to social pressures?

6. How do your kids express themselves? Are they introverted or extroverted? How would you rate their problem-solving skills?

7. How would you describe your child's peer group? Do you approve of his/her friends? Do you know their parents?

8. Are you familiar with your child's unique way of expressing sadness or depression? How well does h/she handle stress or change?

9. Has your child tried alcohol or drugs? What types of substances do you think he/she might have already experimented with?

10. Have you had discussions with your child regarding sex and the potential consequences associated with being in a sexually active relationship?

Chapter 3

Effective Communication

The ability to communicate effectively when discussing challenging and taboo subjects will be one of the most important topics discussed throughout this book. Effective communication fosters the development of a healthy bond between parent and child. Learning ways to expand upon this skill is important on so many levels. Not only does it help to teach children how to be safe, but it also cultivates a lifelong loving and caring relationship. Simply put, healthy and effective dialogue is essential when teaching children how to stay safe in an increasingly dangerous world. In this chapter, we will explore ways to strengthen the relationship between parent and child by focusing specifically on the development of more effective communication strategies.

Parenting can become a very egocentric task in which patterns of communication begin to look more like a lecture series than a relationship defined by the exchange of healthy dialogue. Intensity of emotion is a defining characteristic of adolescence. At times, teenagers may have difficulty containing their emotions and may express their discontent by yelling, crying, or shutting down. As parents, learning how to manage emotional outbursts can mean the difference between a healthy exchange that is solution based versus dialogue that is characterized by arguing, lecturing, or screaming. Though it is difficult, maintaining stability and not contributing to the emotional turmoil will prove to be beneficial. Learning to communicate without negative value judgments or taking outbursts personally can be tremendously helpful in establishing a supportive and loving relationship with your children. The reality is that kids need their parents for guidance, the establishment of healthy boundaries, and, most importantly, effective parenting.

The first step in developing effective communication is to learn how to promote more dynamic exchanges with your children by using active listening skills. The core concept behind active listening is to uncover the emotional content of the exchange. This means that parents must learn how to listen and understand the emotions that their child is trying to express. This concept is extremely important because it helps to foster trust and understanding between parent and child.

So many times within our private practices, we hear parents stress their frustration regarding their inability to engage in any meaningful dialogue with their children. We often hear parents make comments such as, "Whenever I ask my child about school, all they say is it was fine or good. Then they just put their headphones back on and tune me right out." This often causes frustration and allows the child to distance himself from his mother or father. Let's be realistic, it is very easy for kids to tune out their parents by answering with simple yes-or-no responses. One of the most simple and effective ways to break this type of communication is by implementing open-ended questions in the dialogue. Open-ended questions are posed in a manner that stimulates conversation. Instead of asking, "Did you have a good day?" (which is a close-ended question), you could say, "Tell me three things that happened in school today." This type of questioning requires a more engaged and detailed response. Open-ended questions can also be implemented when discussing weekend plans or any other social engagement. Basically, open-ended questions provide more significant conversations simply by not giving kids a way to shut down communication and detach from dialogue.

It is possible, of course, that your child decides not to respond at all and just detaches completely from the conversation. This can happen for any number of reasons, including being tired, having a bad day, or even just the expression of overt disrespect. For any parent, this may cause an increase in frustration and anger. If this is the case, it is important to remember that effective communication cannot be coerced. Instead of engaging in unhealthy dialogue (by yelling, arguing, or screaming), you can take a deep breath and allow him/her some space. If you sense that you are simply being ignored or disrespected, you certainly need to hold the child accountable for his/her inappropriate (or lack of) response in a way that he/she will both hear and respond to in a positive manner. The following is a helpful script that can be used in these types of circumstances.

"It is inappropriate for you not to respond to me when I ask you a question. It is hurtful and disrespectful. I am willing to give you some space, but we need to come up with ways so this does not happen again in the future. We need to be able to talk. Respect is a two-way street. I will show you respect by acknowledging that right now may not be the best time for you to talk. I need for you to show me the same level of respect by coming back to me later and initiating a healthy conversation."

It is surprising to see how often children will come back to you with the desire to talk. It is important to create a relationship in which your children understand that you are genuinely concerned about how they feel, and that you respect them enough to acknowledge a change in their mood or that they might be experiencing other types of emotional turmoil.

Another stumbling block in communication comes from the difficulty that parents face in their attempts to interpret their child's communication patterns. The generation gap can cause confusion and misinterpretation even though the same language is being spoken. An easy way to address this problem is by implementing paraphrasing (another active listening skill) into your repertoire of communication techniques. Paraphrasing is a way for you to put into your own words what your child just expressed to you. Not only does this show him/her that you are paying attention, but it also allows him/her to correct you if you misinterpreted what was said. For instance, if your child describes to you a recent argument or falling out that she had with her best friend at school, you can start your response by saying, "Let me make sure that I'm hearing you correctly. You said." By implementing paraphrasing, you will create an open line of communication based on a give and take between parent and child. Clarifying and repeating to children what you just heard may also give them the opportunity to gain a new perspective on what they just shared. Sometimes hearing you repeat their own story can help them to gain new insight into their ordeal or uncover other ways to tackle the problem at hand. Here is another example of paraphrasing:

> *Jenna came home from a party and started crying. When her father asked what was going on, she replied, "I can't believe Jenny! All she does is spread gossip and say terrible things about people. Today she told Tom that Mandy was sleeping around. When Mandy finds out, she will be devastated." Jenna's father replied, "It sounds like Mandy is spreading lies and rumors about your friends." Jenna then responded, "Yes! How long before she starts doing it with me? What am I supposed to do when she does?"*

Again, paraphrasing will illustrate for your children that you are listening to them and understanding without being judgmental. Had Jenna's father said something like, "Why do you care what Jenny says about your friends?" Jenna likely would have immediately shut down and communication would have ceased.

Communication can also be enriched when we use emotional labeling. This technique will help you to correctly label the emotion that your child is attempting to express. Simply stating "you seem angry" or "it sounds like you are really upset

16

about this" helps to show that you understand what your child is experiencing. When you use emotional labeling, you are also using an active listening skill that helps you to connect with your child without commenting on or judging the validity of her feelings. This will strengthen your relationship and help you to express greater empathy, compassion, and understanding. Using emotionally descriptive words also allows your child to correct you if you are interpreting her words incorrectly. You may hear your child say, "No, Mom, I'm not angry. I'm really sad about all those awful things Jennifer said about me." It is important to remember that you may not understand the gravity of what your child is going through. Though we can conjure up memories about our youth, we quickly forget the intensity of the emotions that we were experiencing at the time. Validating your child's feelings allows her to express any hurt, anger, or frustration that develops from normal adolescent interactions. Using emotional labeling helps to develop an environment in which your child will be more likely to talk with you. This nonjudgmental approach helps to foster greater support and understanding.

Another important active listening skill that can be implemented to help create more effective communication is the use of "I" statements. Though this may seem elementary or a bit cliché, the reality is that "I" statements will contribute to the development of more healthy dialogue. Stating "I feel really upset when you choose to talk back to me in that tone" is quite different from saying "You are really making me angry with your attitude." "You are" statements shut down communication and will put your child in a defensive position. You may be mad, angry, or even infuriated by your child's actions, but shutting down communication will do nothing to resolve the current conflict. "I" statements will allow you to express how you are feeling by using emotionally appropriate descriptors without blaming your child for your current mood. Owning your own emotions will also model the right way to take personal responsibility for how you feel and react to any given situation. It is crucial to remember that as rational and logical beings, we can choose how we react to other people's emotional outbursts.

Chloe came home after curfew on a Friday night. When she walked in the door, both of her parents were waiting for her. When asked why she was late, Chloe said, "I don't know, sometimes people are late." Chloe's father then replied "Chloe, when you disregard our rules, it makes me feel like you don't care for or respect me as your father. What can I do to help you understand that you have a curfew because it helps to keep you safe?" Hopefully, Chloe's parents have already discussed with

Chloe what the consequences will be when she breaks her curfew.

By using an "I" statement, Chloe's father attempts to use an active listening technique to keep Chloe from becoming defensive. He has also set up a dialogue in which all three people are participants instead of Mom and Dad simply lecturing Chloe (which she will not hear) or imposing sanctions that she may not understand or with which she may disagree. In this situation, Chloe is invited to take responsibility for her actions and to be a part of the solution instead of immediately being labeled as the problem.

Another question that is important to ask yourself is, "What am I teaching my kids?" Do you scream at them and then expect them not to yell when they are angry? Do you lecture them while insisting that they learn how to be better listeners? Do you disregard their feelings and then expect them to be more sensitive to others? This type of communication is confusing and counterproductive. Asking yourself "What am I teaching my kids?" as well as "What do I want to teach my kids?" will help you to be more purposeful in your interactions, and increase the likelihood that you will be modeling healthy and appropriate behavior. It also helps you to feel more in control of the dialogue that is being exchanged, as well as the tone being used.

To improve upon effective communication strategies, it is essential to have insight into the type of responses or reactions that cause a breakdown in healthy dialogue. When we develop patterns of communication and behaviors defined by lecturing, yelling, or arguing, effective communication and problem solving will suffer. Maladaptive approaches such as these will contribute to a one-sided and ineffective communication style. With all of the challenges facing kids and parents, relying on solid communication techniques to modify behavior and improve relationships is extremely important. One of the pitfalls that can contribute to these ineffective approaches occurs when parents cannot manage their own expression of emotions. If you are aware that your emotional level is high and altering your ability to engage rationally, you must implement strategies to decrease your agitation. Deep breathing, progressive relaxation, or simply finding a few minutes of peace and quiet before you engage in a challenging conversation can make the difference between a positive exchange that is meaningful and helpful as opposed to one characterized by anger and frustration.

In private practice, we have the opportunity to help individuals, couples, and families learn new ways to address and overcome the conflicts that disrupt a tranquil home life. In couples counseling, one of the most successful and eye-opening interventions is to remind parents that the behaviors exhibited in front of their kids will shape and influence how their children will act within their own relationships. I can recall a father who turned pale white when I asked him if he would want his precious daughter to bring home a man like himself. Would he want her boyfriend, fiancé, or husband to talk to his daughter the way he talks to his wife? Would he be comfortable hearing this man degrade or attack her in front of her own children, family, or friends? In therapy, confronting these maladaptive patterns of behavior and communication can help a person gain insight into the long-term consequences of the behaviors that he/she is modeling for his/her children. It is so important to remember that kids are like sponges. They absorb all that is happening around them. For kids, their parents' relationship is the standard for how they will perceive the way in which couples are supposed to act toward one another. Behaviors exhibited within the household will surely resonate and shape relationships for the next generation.

It takes a significant effort to enhance the language patterns that define communication within your household. Improved communication relies primarily on you, the parent, taking personal responsibility for the way in which you interact with your kids or any other member of your family. If you are trying to get your children to hear you, then it is imperative for you to say things in a way that they will understand. This can be especially challenging when children are responding to your attempts at improving communication by being disrespectful, irritable, or manipulative. When this occurs (and with teenagers it is almost guaranteed that it will), it is very important to manage your own frustration and anger. Yet, if you fully expect that this will happen at some point, you can then anticipate and alter your own reaction by playing the situation out in your mind. By decreasing your own stress and frustration, effective communication strategies become much more of a reality. Remember that you can be firm and loving at the same time. It is extremely important for children to see their parents actually parenting. It shows them that not only do you care and love them, but also that you are invested in helping them to overcome any problems that they may be experiencing. You do not have to be perfect as a parent; just consistent, with realistic expectations and good problem-solving skills. Consistency is imperative with regard to discipline and setting up expectations within the household. A permissive parenting style that allows your children to rule the roost is ineffective and dangerous. Research within the mental health field has shown that parents who implement more consistent approaches to discipline and establish stable, realistic expectations raise healthy and well-adjusted teens (Haynie, 1999.) Consistency is such a vital aspect of parenting simply because kids need to know what is expected of them and the consequences associated with any negative behaviors. If we take this concept one step further, we can see that consistency in the way in which parents react to their own emotional turmoil also plays a tremendous role in maintaining a healthy and safe home life. For example, if your children never know from one moment to the next what kind of mood you are in, what is punishable and what is not, or how you will react to a mistake or bad news, they cannot possibly feel safe. Kids need to trust their parents and, in return, parents must do all that they can to create an environment in which the foundation is based on compassion, love, and understanding.

Inconsistency is problematic when it comes to maintaining a healthy household. Your children interpret your behavior and moods no differently from the way you do theirs. Part of the human experience is interpretation of behavior and analysis of social cues. If spilled milk today leads to rage, your child will assume that this is the standard response for a mistake or accident. If the same accident tomorrow leads to a shrug of the shoulders and "That's okay, accidents happen," confusion will be the norm, and this will create an anxiety-provoking environment for your kids ("Why did I get screamed at yesterday but not today?").

The challenges associated with raising children are vast. The more active a role parents play, the greater the payoff. Knowing that you are doing all that you can to raise healthy and well-adjusted kids will hopefully help you to sleep better at night. Good communication, consistency, and love will be the keys to overcoming many of the obstacles and challenges present within twenty-first-century families.

Let us review some of the key concepts discussed regarding communication and the development of intervention strategies based on healthy and productive dialogue.

1. Communication is the thread that connects all interventions and provides the foundation for a healthy bond between parent and child.

2. The first step in developing effective communication is learning how to promote more dynamic exchanges by using active listening skills. The core concept behind active listening is to learn how to uncover the actual emotional content of the exchange.

3. Open-ended questions are expressed in a manner that stimulates conversation. Instead of asking, "How was school?" (which is a close-ended question), you could say, "Tell me

three things that happened in school today." This type of questioning requires a more engaged and detailed response.

4. Paraphrasing is a way for you to put into your own words what your child just expressed to you. Not only does this show him/her that you are paying attention, but it also allows him/her to correct you if you misinterpreted what was said.

5. Emotional labeling will help you to correctly label the emotion that your child is trying to express. When you use emotional labeling, you are also using an active listening skill that helps you to connect with your child without commenting on or judging the validity of her feelings. This will strengthen your relationship and help you to express greater empathy, compassion, and understanding.

6. "I" statements will allow you to express how you are feeling by using emotionally appropriate descriptors without blaming your child for your current mood or agitation. Owning your own emotions will also model the right way to take personal responsibility for how you feel and react to any given situation.

7. If you are aware that your emotional level is high or impacting your ability to engage rationally, you must implement

strategies to decrease your arousal. Deep breathing, progressive relaxation or simply finding a few minutes of peace and quiet before you engage in a challenging conversation can make the difference between a positive exchange that is meaningful and helpful versus one characterized by anger and frustration.

8. Consistency is imperative when establishing expectations within the household. Research within the metal health field has shown that parents who implement more consistent approaches to discipline and establish stable expectations raise healthy and well-adjusted teens (Haynie 1999). Consistency is such a vital aspect of parenting simply because kids need to know what is expected of them and the consequences associated with negative behaviors.

9. The challenges associated with raising children are vast. The more active a role parents play, the greater the payoff.

Chapter 4

Discipline and Cooperative Problem Solving

When discussing unconditional love and support with parents, a common fear expressed is that this approach will create spoiled, entitled, and narcissistic teens. Fortunately, exploring the differences between overindulgence, discipline, and unconditional love and support usually helps to clarify any confusion regarding these concepts. Parents who provide unconditional love while using discipline effectively and establishing clear rules and expectations do not create a narcissistic personality. Well-adjusted teens who understand the consequences associated with their choices have a much easier time coping with the chaos of adolescence. We know that teens will make mistakes, some within the normal range of development and others with more drastic consequences. To effectively discipline, we need to effectively communicate. Rules, expectations, and dialogue should be the cornerstone of every interaction that involves discipline for inappropriate behavior. "Discipline" and "punishment" are terms that seem interchangeable but, in reality, are actually quite different. Discipline works to help teens to understand the reason why their decision-making process led them down a problematic path, and, most importantly, how to learn from their mistakes. Punishment works by teaching your children to make sure that the next time they make a poor decision, they better not get caught.

By using unconditional love as a guiding principle within the family system, parents can establish a safe and supportive environment that cultivates personal growth and strong moral character. Support and love within a family can help to strengthen a child's ego and provide a sense of safety when dealing with all the pressures of adolescence. Parents have the responsibility to encourage self-discovery by reinforcing their children's strengths and openly discussing the issues with which they struggle in their lives. As human beings, we all have limitations, and it is foolish not to accept this and teach that many deficits can be overcome by hard work and perseverance. Competency and progress come from taking a realistic view of who we are as unique individuals. When discussing limitations in a supportive and loving environment, personal growth, insight, and coping skills all improve. These are lifelong lessons that will help tremendously as adolescents move toward adulthood.

If children grow up in environments in which they receive negative, degrading, or demeaning messages, they will develop insecurities and devalue themselves as persons. This puts them more at risk for being taken advantage of and preyed upon. A good example of this can be seen when a young adolescent girl is "talked into" having sex just to feel accepted or loved. If people feel insecure, they are more willing to let go of their own moral code and allow others to exploit them strictly because they do not like themselves or believe that they have any self-worth. Whenever possible, parents need to ask themselves two questions:

1. What am I teaching?

2. What message am I sending?

When individuals have an innate sense that they have value and worth, they will make decisions based not only on self-preservation, but also personal growth and development. Providing an environment that allows discourse and joint decision making is nothing less than empowering. If you create a family life in which your children are willing to discuss challenging (and even taboo) topics, you reinforce the importance of dialogue and healthy decision making by engaging in thought-provoking exchanges that support growth and improve insight.

At its root, discipline always provides a teachable moment to both parent and child. In its most effective form, discipline is directly linked with teaching versus punishment and punitive responses. Effective discipline reinforces ethical and moral behavior and helps to teach that all behaviors have consequences. Consequences can be seen strictly as punishment, yet this is only a portion of the equation. Consequences can be far reaching and are not only limited to the loss of privilege or freedom. The teachable moment comes from connecting the action or behavior to the consequences that can occur emotionally, socially, and even spiritually. Parents have a responsibility to emphasize and express (in a manner that the teenage mind can comprehend) why the behavior is inappropriate and maladaptive. While working with parents in family therapy, a common mistake that often occurs in regard to discipline involves consistency. Both parents must be in agreement concerning discipline. This is not only true for two-parent households, but also for divorced parents who share custody and are co-parenting. When parents disagree on expectations or consequences, their child's behavior will not be altered. Teens will exploit any inconsistencies in parenting and mitigate any discipline or punishment by manipulating the dynamic and exposing the inconsistency in parenting approaches. Without consistency, you cannot expect any changes in behavior, because the expectations or standards are shifting.

Another consequence of inconsistency is that it provides an environment in which people in general, and teens and children specifically, feel unsafe. When teens are not certain which parent they will meet when they make a mistake, it creates a sense of anxiety and fear that can negatively affect their self-esteem as well as their decision making. When an individual spills the proverbial milk and isn't sure whether she will be greeted with "What in the world is wrong with you? Why are you the clumsiest, most worthless person on earth?" or "It is okay, accidents happen. Let me help you clean it up," it creates an environment that is chaotic and unsure. Consistency is a key component to effective discipline.

It is ironic that effective parenting strategies share many of the same techniques used by hostage negotiators during crisis situations. In parenting and hostage negotiations, effective com-

munication, active listening skills, the establishment of negotiable and nonnegotiable rules, and cooperative decision making
are the principles that lead to successful outcomes. Nonnegotiable rules should be specific and consistent. Similarities between hostage negotiations and parenting include the first two
nonnegotiable rules: no violence, and no drugs/alcohol. For
example, if you turn a blind eye to intoxication on a Friday
night, or if you find drug paraphernalia in your child's room,
you cannot be surprised when the behavior escalates and leads
to a severe consequence (including heavy drug use, academic
problems, acting out, etc.). Violence (physical, emotional, or
verbal) must also be nonnegotiable. All members of the family
must be treated with dignity and respect. This includes interactions between siblings, parents, and any other person living
under the same roof. Arguments and disagreements will occur,
but they do not have to be marred by shaming, disparaging
remarks, or personal attacks that are hurtful and damaging.
Remember, role modeling plays a key role in parenting, and if
you engage in emotionally abusive or degrading behavior during
arguments, you are establishing the type of behavior that will
be considered acceptable and expected within the walls of your
home. School attendance should also be on the nonnegotiable
list. Chronic absenteeism and tardiness can lead to problematic

behaviors because of a lack of supervision and blatant disregard for societal norms and expectations. As a family, you can certainly add to the list with things specific to your family, such as church attendance or even daily exercise. Whatever you choose, the most important component is that the rules are concise and consistent.

Conflicts, disagreements, and arguments will occur between parents and their children. This is a normal part of the maturation process, and it has probably been happening since the first families began to inhabit the earth. The parent-child dynamic in any household will shift during adolescence. In a healthy and stable family, the conflicts are manageable and contribute to growth and insight. The challenge for parents is learning how to use effective communication and active listening to maintain rules and boundaries, to discuss challenging topics openly, to discipline appropriately, and to provide an environment that fosters growth and a strong sense of self. A specific, concrete, and helpful tool that aids in this development of a healthy family dynamic is learning how to engage in cooperative decision making instead of preaching, demanding, or forcing compliance when discussing negotiable topics. Power struggles will not work in initiating any long-term behavioral change and will only create an environment in which maladaptive patterns of behavior are reinforced strictly because they differ from a parent's position. From a strategic parenting standpoint, it is ineffective to use rigid problem-solving techniques when trying to find alternatives or alter negative behaviors. Rigid problem solving reinforces that each side (parent and child) has a position on which he/she is unwilling to compromise. All this does is create a stalemate that fuels the fire of deceit, disagreement, and conflict. An alternative to this approach is learning how to use cooperative decision making by searching for mutually beneficial solutions that decrease conflict. Cooperative decision making helps the family to examine problems together and allows for both perspectives to be thoroughly explored. So how is this done? Let us look at a four-step approach that shows how to implement cooperative decision making instead of rigid problem solving.

Step 1: Move Away from Emotion and Toward Rationality: Cooperative decision making begins by detaching from emotionally clouded thinking and moving toward rationality. If your decision making is influenced by high emotion, it will be ineffective because it reinforces rigid problem solving and focuses on emotion instead of solutions or compromise. Learning how not to react to emotionally charged discussions takes practice and repetition. A calm and rational mind allows you to think clearly and detach from any emotionally fueled behavior.

Step 2: Listen and Acknowledge: Part of the maturation process for all teens is finding their own voice and developing a sense of self. This can be used to your advantage when implementing cooperative decision making by sincerely listening to the content of what is being said, as well as the emotion that is being expressed. Allow their feelings to be expressed and, most importantly, heard. Show empathy and stay focused on the topic being discussed and explored. When a person feels as if someone is listening, the dynamic shifts to a more effective and appropriate dialogue. Hostility decreases as rationality increases. Arguments are destructive. Listening decreases tension and contributes tremendously to compromise.

Step 3: Shift from Rigid Problem Solving to Cooperative Decision Making: After listening and acknowledging, the next step is to move toward a more solution-based approach. Search for common ground and ask for input regarding compromise. Allow children to feel as if they are part of the solution and that they have a voice during this problem-solving phase. Asking for feedback is the key to this step. Build on their input and bolster the ideas or solutions that you find the most constructive or mutually beneficial. You need to actively involve them in finding solutions so that they can buy into the process and move away from resistance. Integrate their ideas into a solution that you find acceptable. Remember that you can always find common ground, even if it is only a sliver. Start from there and move forward.

Step 4: Overcome Resistance and Establish a Firm Boundary: If your teen is unwilling to discuss, compromise, or search for resolution, you must let him/her know the consequences associated with his/her unwillingness to engage in cooperative decision making. This is not a threat; it is just reality. It should also be a part of your discipline plan. There exists a power differential between parents and children. This is normal, beneficial, and appropriate. Expressing your willingness to discuss topics is essential. If children are not willing to talk, the consequences need to be consistent and explicit.

Cooperative decision making can be used with negotiable topics. For instance, let us look at a common conflict that occurs between parents and teens: curfew. For the sake of the example, let us say that an 11 p.m. curfew has been set as the standard in the Smith household. Nancy Smith (age fifteen) has been invited to a homecoming dance at her high school. After the dance, a group of Nancy's friends (including her date) plan on going to a late-night diner for food. Nancy asks her parents if she is allowed to stay out later than her normal curfew. Her parents have two choices. They can take a hard line and rigid approach and state that the curfew has been established for a reason and that Nancy needs to be home by 11 p.m. without exception (this type of approach would reinforce rigid problem solving). The second option for the Smith family is to discuss with Nancy their concerns and expectations regarding staying out late, and to ask her specifically what she could do to make them more willing to alter her curfew time (call or text when she leaves the dance, when she gets to the diner, and when she leaves). This stimulates conversation and allows both parties to discuss the issue at hand. It further models for Nancy and teaches her how to make effective and appropriate decisions as she moves from adolescence into adulthood. By using cooperative decision making, both Nancy and her parents can discuss their concerns, expectations, and desires. Nancy's parents can certainly establish that the change in curfew is for this special event only and will not be altered for most normal weekend nights. The second approach acknowledges that flexibility is a part of the family dynamic, and that solutions can be found together. It also establishes more trust and provides Nancy with the opportunity to make good decisions. Implementing effective discipline strategies that can successfully curb problematic behavior takes hard work and consistency. These strategies are a crucial part of the child-rearing process because "discipline teaches moral and social standards, and it should protect children from harm by teaching what is safe while guiding them to respect the rights and property of others" (Banks 2002, p. 1,448). When used from a supportive and loving approach, discipline can teach as well as alter problematic behavior. Discipline does not need to take the form of verbal or corporal punishment to be effective. Degrading remarks, shame, or even physical strikes will not alter long-range behavior and often reinforces violence (verbal or physical) as a way to deal with stress or conflict. "Studies have shown an association between corporal punishment received as a child and anger that persists into adulthood, increasing the likelihood that those persons will use physical punishment with their own children" (Banks 2002, p. 1,450). Role modeling violence only perpetuates destructive discipline and reinforces impulsivity, which leads to more conflict and escalating troublesome behavior.

Another successful parenting strategy is to allow your teens as much freedom as possible within the bounds that you have set as a family. This includes knowing when and which battles to fight. Parents are not a fountain of endless energy. Parents get tired and parents make mistakes. This becomes important to remember, because these mistakes can seem overwhelming at times. Acknowledging your mistakes is an excellent opportunity to show your children that mistakes are also normal and natural. Modeling how people learn from their mistakes can be a valuable lesson for your teen. Choose your battles carefully, and remember that you cannot win them all. Make it a goal to win the important ones.

Nonabusive discipline strategies include the implementation of natural and logical consequences as a way to hold teens responsible for the breaking of household rules or expectations. Natural consequences teach how choices affect outcome and allow the experience of breaking a rule or expectation to dictate the consequence. For example, if a student fails an academic class, the repercussions should be summer school. All too often, parents will advocate relentlessly for their child so that he/she does not have to attend. Many teachers, guidance counselors, and administrators have heard parents make comments such as, "We have a summer vacation planned. John can't be in summer school and miss this trip." Natural consequences would dictate that John does miss the trip and that he is held accountable for failing his history class. If you enable John's undesirable behavior by not allowing the education system to hold him responsible for his failure, all you are doing is reinforcing patterns that teach limited responsibility and detachment from consequences. Logical consequences are usually established by parents and directly relate to privileges within the household. "The principle behind logical consequences is that privilege must be earned and maintained through responsible action" (Romaine 2007, p. 8). Privilege can take many forms, including access to technology (gaming devices, cell phones, computers), time spent with friends, or any other hobby or event that has value for your teen.

Positive reinforcement is another critical aspect of effective parenting and discipline. Parental attention and healthy and productive feedback help to build ego strength and confidence. The main premise behind positive reinforcement is to focus on good behavior and to provide feedback for desirable and healthy choices. Rewards can take many forms, including verbal praise and acknowledgement, extra privileges, or even material goods. For positive reinforcement to be most effective, the reward has to be provided following the desired response. This may be challenging for parents, because it is too easy to focus on negative behavior and to forget the importance of reinforcing actions that are desirable. Focusing on positive reinforcement can be a reminder to move away from negativity and toward a healthy (and more successful) approach to parenting. In terms of material goods, positive reinforcement cannot be given out with reckless abandon. Positive reinforcement differs significantly from overindulgence. Providing material goods to curb or influence behavior will not be an effective long-term parenting strategy. It will help to create a manipulative child who will be motivated only when provided with an external stimulus (e.g., new laptop, cell phone, car, etc.). The long-term consequences of this approach can contribute to an addiction to consumerism, material goods, and spending. Materialism teaches kids to be driven by marketing companies and advertisers. It does not build self-esteem or confidence. All too often in our private practice, we hear parents in family therapy make comments such as, "Look, if you just pass your classes, I'll buy you a new cell phone." As therapists, we understand that parents want the best for their child and are willing to try anything to curb or alter behavior; yet, this strategy is ineffective and only reinforces materialism.

Overindulgence goes hand in hand with consumerism. Consumerism is a worldwide cultural phenomenon that uses marketing and advertising to make every possible person on earth a consumer of a particular good or service. Marketing works, and its effects are far reaching. This explains why corporations are willing to spend millions of dollars per second to push their product during a Super Bowl commercial. Further proof can be found at any mall across America when the latest and greatest gadget is being released to the public. The lines begin days in advance, and the number of consumers waiting can be staggering. "[An] overwhelming level of social stimulation inundates families today. Marketers over the globe are targeting children as influential vehicles of marketing and prospective adult consumers. These children have their own purchase power and influence over the buying decisions of parents. Children contribute in the decision-making process of various products in families" (Mahima 2008, p. 32). The overindulgent parent provides material goods as an alternative to parenting. Take away the power from marketing firms and advertisers by reinforcing desirable behaviors with love and praise.

Discipline relies on rationality, effective communication, cooperative decision making, and active parenting. Discipline comes from a place of love and concern. Discipline incorporates teaching with positive messages. Disagreements and even the breaking of household rules and expectations are a normal part of development. When addressed appropriately, they provide an opportunity to teach and show love and support to your child. Discourse does not have to cause a crisis within the family structure. Active parenting and open dialogue ultimately help to curb and alter maladaptive patterns of behavior and reinforce growth and improved insight.

Let us review some of the key concepts discussed regarding discipline and cooperative problem solving:

1. To discipline effectively, we need to communicate effectively. Rules, expectations, and dialogue should be the cornerstone of every interaction that involves discipline for inappropriate behavior.

2. Whenever possible, parents need to ask themselves two questions: "What am I teaching?" and "What message am I sending?"

3. At its root, discipline always provides a "teachable moment" to both parent and child. In its most effective form, discipline is linked directly with teaching versus punishment and punitive responses.

4. Teens will exploit any inconsistencies in parenting and mitigate any discipline or punishment by manipulating the dynamic and exposing the inconsistency in parenting approaches.

5. Arguments and disagreements will occur, but they do not have to be marred by shaming, disparaging remarks, or personal attacks that are hurtful and damaging. Role modeling plays a key role in parenting, and if you engage in emotionally abusive or degrading behaviors during arguments, you are establishing the type of behavior that will be considered acceptable and expected.

6. From a strategic parenting standpoint, it is ineffective to use rigid problem-solving techniques when trying to find alternatives or alter negative behaviors. Rigid problem solving reinforces that each side (parent and child) has a position on which he/she is unwilling to compromise. All this does is create a stalemate that fuels the fire of deceit, disagreement, and conflict.

7. Cooperative decision making helps the family to examine problems together and allows for both perspectives to be thoroughly explored. Here are the four steps:

   (a) Move away from emotion and toward rationality.

   (b) Listen and acknowledge.

   (c) Shift from rigid problem solving to cooperative decision making.

   (d) Overcome resistance and establish a firm boundary.

8. Modeling how people learn from their mistakes can be a valuable lesson for your teen. Choose your battles carefully and remember that you cannot win them all. Make it a goal to win the important ones.

9. Natural consequences teach how choices affect outcome and allow the experience of breaking a rule or expectation to dictate the consequence.

10. Logical consequences are established by parents and directly relate to privileges within the household. Privileges must be earned and maintained by engaging in appropriate behaviors.

Chapter 5

Cyberbullying Vignette

In a typical suburban neighborhood in the Midwest, two childhood friends became estranged as their friendship fell victim to the typical strife that affects so many pre-adolescent teenagers. In the past, when two friends became entangled in conflict, recourse usually included making snide remarks about each other in school or perhaps spreading rumors among their peer group. Unfortunately for these two girls, life became much more complicated. As the story of their relationship unfolded, a MySpace account and cyberbullying would come to define their shattered friendship and alter their lives forever.

The story of Mary, a cyberbullying victim, represents the fears and concerns that many parents have regarding their children and social networking sites. These sites can provide an avenue via which a tidal wave of negative attention can cause severe emotional distress in a child. Mary was a fourteen-year-old girl with a MySpace account. From the news reports, her parents initially took many precautions to monitor her usage and to make sure that she was engaging in appropriate and safe behavior on this social networking site. Over the course of time, Mary was contacted by a boy named "Tom." Tom wasn't real; his profile, his interests, and even his personality were created by a former friend of Mary's. The two friends had a falling out and were no longer close. Tom was designed specifically to attract Mary and to have her engage in an online romantic relationship with him. He appeared to be perfect. They shared many of the same interests and seemed to enjoy each other's company. After several weeks of correspondence, Mary perceived that they had become very close. Perception and reality became blurred. Mary was completely unaware that Tom did not even exist outside of cyberspace. The relationship between the two began to shift as Tom's behavior was manipulated to hurt Mary. Accusations were made, words were exchanged, and Mary became very distressed. Her pain and emotional turmoil did not escape her parents' attention, but the severity of it did. Neither her mother nor father was aware of the manipulation and deceit that was being perpetrated against their daughter online. Though initially diligent with their online restrictions, time and frequency of use without any trouble led to a decrease in monitoring. After spending several hours on her MySpace page being harassed and bullied by her "friends," Mary went up to her bedroom and decided that life was no longer worth living. She made a noose, tied it around her neck, and ended her young life.

Although many of the specifics of this tragedy are in dispute and have been argued in a court of law, there are certain elements that are consistent within many cyberbullying cases. Mary had an online relationship with a person who, in reality, did not exist. Though the lines of her reality became blurred, the one consistent fact is that Mary thought that "Tom" cared for her and wanted to be her friend. Mary was searching for acceptance and companionship. This does not differ from the wants and desires of the majority of kids.

Sadly, Mary was being bullied in a forum that provides immediate and anonymous attacks. This anonymity only serves to make the attacks more hateful. Posts that state that a person is worthless, unhip, or a loser can be just as harmful as being told to your face between classes or on the playground that you are a social outcast. The cyberbully does not even have to look into the eyes of his/her victim or see the painful response that the verbal attack caused. Proximity is not relevant. The bully can live as close as next door or thousands of miles away and still actively participate in rumors, innuendo, and verbal assaults without fear of retribution. In many ways, cyberbullying can be more damaging and dangerous than the bullying of yesteryear. When unhealthy relationships develop in an online forum, self-esteem can be attacked and shattered, causing severe and dire consequences.

Chapter 6

Internet Safety

The challenges and obstacles that occur during the normal stages of adolescent development can be difficult for even the best-prepared child. The desire to fit into the cool crowd or at least avoid being a social outcast is tremendously important for most kids. Even for many adults, the struggles that they experienced during adolescence can be brought to mind with minimal prodding. Most can recall a time when they were the subject of a schoolyard rumor or when they were tormented at the hands of a local bully. As trying as these experiences were, technology has intensified the challenges that adolescents face and significantly altered the traumatic effects that they can have on the maturing child. In the past, rumors were usually spread within a single school or neighborhood. The Internet and social networking sites such as MySpace and Facebook have changed the nature of the rumor mill by infinitely increasing its reach and the longevity of its cruelty.

Anyone who has ever spent time with a teenager and a mirror knows firsthand how important it is for him/her to look good and fit in with his/her peer group. Magazine racks are littered with current fashion trends that dictate how kids are supposed to dress, wear their hair, and which body parts to pierce or tattoo. Most teenagers are driven by the desire to fit in socially and not stand out from the crowd. They begin to see themselves as the center of the universe, and this egocentric view becomes a primary part of the maturing adolescent. This is healthy because the teen is in the process of developing a whole slew of new mental abilities and insight into the inner workings of society and the world. When an adolescent states, "Everybody is going to laugh at me," or, "Mom, you have no idea what everyone is going to say about this," they believe that this is the case. The term "imaginary audience" has been coined to describe this, and it is basically at the root of why teenagers are so self-conscious. If teenagers spend all day thinking about themselves and how they fit into the outside world, then surely, in their minds, all those around them are also thinking about them, too. Now more than ever, technology and the Internet can reinforce this flawed thinking. Suddenly, the whole world (or at least those whom they consider relevant members of their peer group) is reading about them on a blog or, even worse, seeing pictures or videos of them posted on a social networking site. This is why the effects of cyberbullying can be so detrimental and even dangerous to your child.

In 2006, the Centers for Disease Control and Prevention (http://goo.gl/JQ9Y2) defined electronic aggression as "any kind of aggression perpetrated through technology — any type of harassment or bullying (teasing, telling lies, making fun of someone, making rude or mean comments, spreading rumors, or making threatening or aggressive comments) that occurs through e-mail, a chat room, instant messaging, a website (including blogs), or text messaging." The variety of methods used is expansive and extensive, and its reach endless. Online rumors are like a slow-moving hurricane that gains strength and power as it crawls over a warm body of water, eventually hitting land and leaving a wake of destruction in its path. Rumors spread violently through chat rooms and social networking sites and build up speed and momentum with every keyboard click. Because of the digital nature of these types of disparaging attacks, they are difficult to stop and alter once they have hit cyberspace.

The cruelty and severity of online attacks can generate a tremendous amount of distress and hurt for a teen being tormented in cyberspace. Cyberbullies can hide behind user names where anonymity allows them to be cruel and hurtful. They do not have to obey the normal social cues or etiquette that dictates human interactions, and they can attack without hesitation. A bully has technology on his/her side and is able to generate a tremendous feeling of power that comes from his/her manipulation of stories and spreading of hurtful rumors. It is important for parents to remember that text messaging plays a crucial role in this type of harassment. It is now commonplace to share videos, texts, and pictures with everyone in your social network. This is why it is imperative for intervention strategies to be directed toward all types of communication devices and formats. We are not suggesting that social networking should be avoided or that it is inherently flawed; simply that it is very powerful and care should be taken with this form of communication.

At times, the generation gap can cause a breakdown in basic communication between parents and their kids. To many parents, it may seem that their teenager is speaking a completely different language marked by slang, acronyms, and pop culture references. Because of this, focusing on improving your listening skills is of vital importance. This becomes extremely relevant when it comes to understanding how your child is interacting with others online. To gain insight into your children's online behavior, you can ask them for a tutorial into their cyberworld. Have them show you the most relevant sites, and see who they are communicating with, and how. Even if they are not disclosing all of the sites or networks that they normally frequent, you can at least see firsthand how they are using the web. Be genuine when you probe regarding how their friends also use these sites. Ask about cyberbullying and if they have witnessed, been a victim of, or even participated in this act. Learn from them and use this knowledge to create a healthy dialogue based on trust and openness. Do not hesitate to discuss the real and present dangers that lurk in cyberspace. Your child needs to know that you can handle the realities of his/her life and that you are willing to provide him/her with support and guidance.

Do not be afraid to discuss depression or any other emotions that your child might be experiencing. To keep your child safe, you must know how he/she is coping emotionally. It is extremely important for you, the parent, to monitor your child's mood and to be aware of any expression of distress. If there is a change in your child's mood, you must address it with him/her in a compassionate and caring manner. Healthy communication is essential and can prove to be your most effective intervention. Almost all parental exchanges can be improved upon if you listen to what your child is saying and, more importantly, is displaying by his actions. Remember, behavior rarely lies.

During times of increased stress, your child needs your support and love. Being a parent is a difficult and labor-intensive job. Observation of body language along with verbal cues becomes a key component in the exchange of information. Are his/her shoulders slumped? Is he/she avoiding eye contact? Does he/she seem to be carrying stress in his/her facial expressions? These are signs that allow you to better understand what is happening to your teen emotionally. This differs from just simple listening because it provides you, the parent, with insight into the emotional content of the exchange. This strategy may take time to develop, but it is crucial for strengthening the parent-child bond.

As a family unit, an open and honest discussion regarding social networking sites needs to occur. Rules and boundaries must be established prior to the development of a personal social network page. As a parent, your rules must be concrete, and the consequences for breaking them must be clear and firm. For example, the content of the page, including all pictures, videos, or other personal identifiers, must be approved prior to posting. Parents need to stress that there is absolutely no sharing of personal information (telephone numbers, home address, Social Security number, etc.) on this site. This also holds true for any meetings initiated by strangers who have responded to a posting or shared information. Even though kids often believe that they are invincible, you need to share with them the harsh realities and types of predatory behaviors present throughout cyberspace. If you choose to allow your child to participate in a social network, it is of extreme importance that all passwords are shared with you and that the sites are monitored frequently. If you uncover inappropriate content or dialogue, there must be tangible consequences. All rules must be clear and consistent. Ultimately, the goal is to keep your child safe and help him/her to avoid potentially life-altering mistakes. You may be angry or frustrated with his/her behavior, but you must be willing to engage in healthy dialogue. Adolescents need help in developing a deeper understanding of the severe consequences that can occur as a result of their actions. Modeling healthy communication helps them to learn from your example. Let them learn from their mistakes and how to take responsibility for their actions. These lessons, though difficult, will help to guide them along their personal path as they mature and move toward adulthood.

It is important to educate your kids about the online tactics that predators use to lure their victims to a personal meeting. These include efforts to gain their trust while encouraging them to question how much they can trust you. Think of online predators as chameleons who will say and do whatever they need to present themselves as the perfect match for your child. "You're into computers. So am I!" "You don't get along with your parents? Neither do I!" "You don't like school? Me neither!" "Wow, we have so much in common, it would be great to meet you some time." How much of what you just read seems unreasonable? The dialogue seems innocent enough, but we need to remember that the underlying goal of the predator is to befriend and ultimately victimize the child on the other end of cyberspace. Teaching kids to be cognizant of these ploys and tactics will help to increase their awareness and offer them insight into how these predators attract their victims.

Ultimately, the dialogue that occurs between you and your child will be the key component in the development of a safety plan that includes all Internet activity. Becoming tech savvy is just another aspect of good parenting. Technology is extremely user friendly and, with practice, can be easily understood. If you become aware that your child is being cyberbullied, it is important for you to know how to block the attacker from contacting your teen. Usually e-mail accounts, instant messenger links, and social networking sites make this option easy to implement in a few simple steps. Prior to erasing any of these attacks, begin documenting the harassment by making copies of the exchange, and marking the time, date, and site where the attack occurred. If the bullying continues, documentation will be an absolute necessity if it escalates to a point where the authorities are involved. Unfortunately, blocking the attacks is more difficult when they occur in the form of a text message on a cell phone. If this is the method used, documentation is still extremely important, and good record keeping is essential (most bills provide a ledger that includes the length of the call, the frequency, and the origin of the number).

If the bully is attending the same school as your child, do not hesitate to bring this to the school's attention. Anonymity is not always the driving force behind cyberbullying. Cyberbullying can easily be an extension of the taunts and harassment that occur within the hallways of your child's school. If this is the case, advocating for your child is extremely important. By letting the school know what is happening with your teen, the intervention approach can be directed at home and at school. Setting up a meeting with your child, a guidance counselor, and a school administrator to discuss the bullying is a good place to start. Bring any documentation that you have recorded, and stress your concern for your child's safety. If threats of physical violence are being directed at your child, or if he/she has already been assaulted, authorities need to be contacted. We live in a more dangerous age, and the days of a simple schoolyard altercation are long gone. The threats are much more significant and must be treated as such. A timeline of the events, documentation of the bullying, and any other relevant information must be shared. Stress to your teen the importance of being open and honest with the other adults involved in this type of situation. Teens need to know that you are supporting them and that they are doing the right thing. Their embarrassment may make it difficult for them to discuss the harassment. If this is the case, focus on helping them to feel empowered by developing their strength and their willingness to tackle difficult situations. Explain how standing up to a bully by using all of your resources is an adaptive, helpful strategy, and how matching their aggression with aggression only causes the problem to escalate. As parents, empathy, love, and support are some of the most powerful weapons in your arsenal. Although rare is the teen who would admit to needing emotional support from his parents, it is virtually a universal truth that teens do in fact value love and support from their parents more than any other source.

To reiterate, so much of Internet safety will come back to the fundamental communication strategies that define your relationship with your teen. The expectation must be that all interactions that take place via the computer or cell phones are open for parental review. Remember that computer access and cell phones are privileges that kids earn and not a right to be taken for granted. As such, they can be removed at any time by you, the parent. They can also be used in discipline as an effective bargaining tool. Do not hesitate to look at your child's phone and scroll through text messages. When it comes to protecting your family, privacy is extremely limited. Increasing your awareness about how your teen uses technology and how he interacts with others is a tremendous step in the right direction. Monitor his mood and be cognizant of his interactions with friends. Be aware of any changes that seem to be significant in the life of a teenager. Do not hesitate to discuss his problems or what is happening to him socially. Any form of bullying needs to be addressed and taken seriously. A family approach can make it much more manageable when facing the multitude of challenges that define life in the twenty-first century.

The following is a list of strategies and interventions that can help your teen to successfully avoid becoming the victim of cyberbullying.

1. As a culture, we are so distracted by outside influences that our normal communication habits have been greatly altered. From text messages to e-mails, language has been

watered down to acronyms and sentence fragments. Parents need to listen to the subtleties expressed by their children and teach them by example the importance of healthy dialogue. Trust is the foundation and must be developed to provide a safe environment in which children can talk openly.

2. Parents need to be familiar with the technology being used by the modern American teen. If you are unaware of what is at your child's disposal, you will have no way to monitor and supervise. If you are less than tech savvy, a simple solution may be to remove the computer from your child's bedroom and place it in a common area within the house.

3. A bully has technology on his/her side and is able to generate a tremendous amount of power that comes from his manipulation of stories and the spreading of hurtful rumors or personal attacks. It is important for parents to remember that text messaging plays a crucial role in this type of harassment. It is now commonplace to share videos, texts, and pictures with everyone in your social network. This is why it is imperative for intervention strategies to be directed toward all types of communication devices and formats.

4. Awareness of how your child is presenting emotionally can

give you insight into what is happening socially. It is extremely important for you, the parent to monitor your child's mood and presentation of distress. Almost all parental exchanges can be improved upon if you listen to what your child is saying and, more importantly, displaying by his actions. Remember, behavior rarely lies.

5. Rules for cell phone and Internet use need to be firmly set in place long before your children begin to encounter situations in which cyberbullying may become an issue. As you set these rules and guidelines, remember to be clear, concise, and, most important, consistent.

Rules for Social Networking Use:

1. As a family unit, an open and honest discussion regarding social networking sites needs to occur. Rules and boundaries must be established prior to the development of a personal social networking page. As a parent, your rules must be concise, and the consequences for breaking those rules must be clear and firm.

2. All posted content must be preapproved (including pictures, videos, or other personal identifiers).

3. All passwords must be known to the parents and are not to be shared with anyone else.

4. We recommend a limit on the number of hours per day/week that your teen is allowed to spend on these sites.

5. Parents need to stress that there is absolutely no sharing of personal information (telephone numbers, home address, Social Security number, etc.) on this site. This also holds true for any meetings initiated by strangers who have responded to a posting or shared information. Even though kids often believe that they are invincible, they need to be aware of the harsh realities and types of predatory behaviors present throughout cyberspace.

6. Anyone under age fourteen should not be on a social networking site.

Guidelines if you suspect bullying:

1. Document the bullying, including dates, times, people, the site, and what specifically was said. You can even take a "screen shot" (a picture of the computer screen) to present to the authorities.

2. If the bully is attending the same school as your child, do not hesitate to bring this to the school's attention. Anonymity is not always the driving force behind cyberbullying. Cyberbullying can easily be an extension of the taunts and harassment that occur within the hallways of your child's

school. If this is the case, advocating for your child is extremely important. By letting the school know what is happening with your teen, the intervention can be directed at home and at school. Setting up a meeting with your child, the guidance counselor, and a school administrator to discuss the bullying is a good place to start.

3. If threats of physical violence are being directed at your child, or if he/she has already been assaulted, authorities need to be contacted. We live in a more dangerous age. The days of simple schoolyard fist fights are long gone and the threats are much more significant.

4. Stress to your teen the importance of being open and honest with the other adults involved in this type of situation. Teens need to know that you are supporting them and that they are doing the right thing. Their embarrassment may make it difficult for them to discuss the harassment. If this is the case, focus on helping them to feel empowered by developing their strength and their willingness to tackle difficult situations

5. Above all, provide empathy, love, and support.

Chapter 7

Avoiding Victimization Vignette

A young girl attended an overnight soccer camp in the hopes of improving her game and having fun with her teammates. When she left for camp, her parents assumed she would be safe, never imagining that she would become a victim of a brutal sexual assault. On that fateful night, she slept alone in her dormitory, unaware that a perpetrator lurked nearby. Unfortunately, this young girl would learn that nightmares don't only occur while we sleep. Instead, the people we fear most can walk through an unlocked door, attack viciously, and commit unspeakable crimes.

How did this series of events unfold? It began with the perpetrator strolling home from a bar with his friends. As he walked along campus, he noticed a light on up in the girls' dormitory.

Fueled by marijuana, alcohol, and bad intentions, his mind ruminated on the potential victim resting quietly in her room. The assailant walked to the entrance of the dormitory and, much to his surprise, saw that the door was unlocked. No supervising staff or security was monitoring the hallways. He entered the building and again was able to get through another unlocked door that allowed him access to the floor where his unsuspecting victim slept. He now had free rein to victimize and attack. All that stood between this man and the young victim was one last unlocked door. With no hesitation, he burst through the door, threatened the child's life, and brutally raped her. After the vicious attack, he threatened her life again and ran from the room. With strength, fortitude, and courage, this brave girl rushed to her camp counselor and told her about the assault. Law enforcement officers raced to the scene. A few months later, the perpetrator was caught, tried, and convicted.

What makes this vignette so important to analyze is the presentation of the perpetrator. This man was working as a coach at the same university. He had a college degree with a good work history. He was out with friends during the night of the rape. When he was arrested, he was able to obtain several letters submitted to the court from members of the community showing shock that this man could be accused of such a crime. He didn't look like a man who attacks and sexually assaults children. He simply didn't fit the profile. To this we say, "what profile?"

Reread the vignette and look for something that could have been done differently to reduce the risk of victimization. Of course, the fact that the dormitory was unlocked from the front door to the dorm room played a significant role in the accessibility to the victim. Parents must take an active role in stressing to their children important lessons such as always locking a door if they are left without supervision. This certainly includes the front door of a home when kids are left alone, and includes never opening a door when a stranger comes knocking. This may sound elementary, but it needs to be stressed time and time again. Simple solutions are often the most successful when deterring crime.

Here is another important lesson learned from this case. How did the assailant choose his victim? In working with inmates, we have learned that opportunity often precedes criminal behavior. Impulsivity and convenience can lead to victimization. Most times, criminals are not plotting and planning their next assault with precision and detail. Instead, crimes are committed when a victim is seen as an easy target. The deviant and distorted mind of a criminal will seek out and exploit the easiest mark when the opportunity presents itself. This chapter will help to uncover the red flags and characteristics exhibited by sex offenders. Developing approaches that focus on safety and deterring victimization should be a crucial part of any parent's assessment of risk.

Chapter 8

Avoiding Sexualized Violence

Children who are sexually abused lose much more than their innocence. Victimization robs them of their faith in adults and destroys their belief that the world is basically a safe place. It causes detachment and can make it difficult for a child to develop healthy relationships with others. A victimized child can experience an increase in mental health symptoms, including depression, anxiety, and posttraumatic stress disorder, and may even engage in sexually inappropriate behaviors (Brier, 1992.) As parents, strategies must be developed that focus on safety, openness, and good communication. Sex offenders prey on the innocent because many children and teens lack the skill set that it takes to understand and interpret the manipulation exhibited by adults (especially when they know the assailant). As parents, learning ways to decrease risk and implement precautionary strategies is essential when confronting predators driven by their desire to sexually exploit and victimize children.

To keep from being overwhelmed by all of the dangers present within the modern world, parents largely function under the illusion of control. Most parents develop psychologically based coping skills naturally, which helps them to raise their children in a complex society. Managing fear and anxiety often occurs through the development of healthy denial. As human beings, it would be extremely difficult to spend the time, energy, or resources that would be necessary to worry about the safety of our children every moment of every day. Even the most proactive parent has to relinquish control and allow a child to interact and engage with the outside world. To manage this fear and relinquish control, parents assume that those adults in charge of watching their children will do so with conviction and care. Psychologically, even allowing kids to attend school, participate in athletics, or spend time with their peers takes the acknowledgment that complete control is unrealistic. Instead, most parents engage in healthy denial because it is necessary and a psychologically sound coping skill.

A vital difference exists, however, between healthy denial and purposeful indifference. Parents need to make every possible effort to ensure safety (and then have trust and faith in those strategies) versus simply hoping that "nothing bad will happen to my child." Parents cannot blindly rely on other people's good natures. A thorough risk assessment includes getting as much history as possible on those individuals in charge of watching your children. Use the Internet, talk to other parents, and ask for references. You need to gather data from a variety of sources to uncover useable information. You must first be as sure as you can reasonably be of others' intentions and good nature before you allow them to be responsible for your kids.

The research and incarceration history of sex offenders continues to emphasize that most offenders are male. The US Department of Justice 2000 reported that 96 percent of all sexual assaults investigated by law enforcement officials involved male offenders. The Department of Justice also reported that juveniles under the age of eighteen initiate 23 percent of the assaults. It appears that younger offenders target younger children. Forty percent of children under the age of six were targeted and victimized by a juvenile sex offender (Department of Justice). Multiple research projects and studies continue to emphasize and drive home the point that friends or family members are responsible for most sexual assaults of children. Rates as high as 90 percent continue to be documented for children abused by an acquaintance (http://goo.gl/JQ9Y2). The Department of Justice also stated that strangers were the offender in just 3 percent of all assaults on children under the age of six, and 5 percent for children ranging from ages six through eleven. Because of these staggering statistics, the responsibility of deciding whom you trust with your child's safety is of vital importance. From the local teenage babysitter to the baseball coach, you must be willing and capable of analyzing their behavior and deciding if they pose any risk to your child. Though this may seem harsh or overprotective, we cannot hide from the reality that abused children are victimized, assaulted, and traumatized by someone deemed trustworthy.

A common misconception is that sexual offenders can be easily identified by their appearance or mannerisms. It is easy to conjure up the image of the latest perpetrator's mug shot profiled on the ten o'clock news. We observe him in his county blues, holding up a sign with his name and prison number on it, and tell ourselves that we would never let someone who looked like that near our kids. What if that same criminal is wearing a well-tailored blue blazer and khaki pants? Would our guard be lowered simply because he appeared well groomed? Unfortunately, the image of the "dirty old man" or "strange uncle" does not always describe those who prey on children and teens. In reality, no profile (psychological or physical) can identify those likely to offend. Research on sex offenders has uncovered the harsh reality that perpetrators come from all walks of life and socioeconomic backgrounds, don't present as psychotic or "crazy," and may have an IQ ranging from extremely intelligent to low functioning (`http://goo.gl/2WweU`). By understanding that sex offenders are not easily identifiable, we can avoid being manipulated because of a faulty assumption that a person poses no risk to our children because he has money, intelligence, or nice clothes. If we assume that risk comes in all shapes and sizes, we are less likely to fall victim to a charismatic offender who is looking for a way to victimize others.

According to the National Incident-Based Reporting System, almost 67 percent of all sexual assault victims were under the age of eighteen. Even more alarming is that amongst those victims, more than half were under the age of twelve (`http://goo.gl/DjEL9`). These statistics are frightening and do not even take into account the crimes that are not reported to the appropriate authorities. In terms of gender, girls are six times more likely to be sexually abused than their male counterparts. Another striking difference between boys and girls is that as boys age, their chance of victimization decreases. For girls, the opposite is true, and their likelihood of being assaulted sexually increases as they move through adolescence (peaking at around the age of fourteen). In terms of the overall numbers of reported cases of sexual assaults against children, one of the leading research resources available online (Crimes Against Children Research Centers) provided the following unfortunate statistics: There a wide variation among estimates of the number of children who are the victims of sexual abuse. This stems from differences in how abuse is defined, the time periods over which studies are conducted, and the understanding that many cases of child sexual abuse are never reported to officials. Thus estimates range from 1.2 victims per $1,000$ to 1.9 victims per thousand in studies focusing on occurrences in one year to between 90 and 280 per thousand found in a survey of adults who experienced some sexual abuse or assault in their childhood.

Even though there is no profile set in stone that can identify sex offenders with absolute certainty, there are some common characteristics that can help in the development of a thorough assessment of risk. Sexually deviant offenders can be broadly classified based primarily on who they choose to victimize and what motivates them to engage in this destructive behavior. Groth 1978 separated sexual offenders into two types: fixated and regressed. Offenders in the fixated group usually present as emotionally immature and are preoccupied with children (the observation of this type of fixation should be an automatic red flag to parents). Their assaults are premeditated and their victims are usually groomed through the development of a superficial relationship based ultimately on how and when they can sexually abuse the vulnerable child. Fixated offenders are more likely to target boys to whom they are not related. In terms of safety, observation regarding adult behavior around children can prove to be extremely important in uncovering any deviance or unhealthy desires exhibited by an adult who spends time with children.

Regressed offenders may not be as overt in their presentation of deviance simply because they tend to have more normal relationships with age-appropriate partners. This can make their detection more challenging. This type of offender is more likely to target a victim whom he knows, and the sexual assault can be triggered by an increase in stress within his life. For parents, it is important to be cognizant of any changes in behavior exhibited by friends, family, or acquaintances that trigger a fixation on your child. With regressed offenders, their deviance is impulsive (a crime of opportunity) and they are more likely to victimize girls.

Sex offending is not always a crime motivated by lack of judgment or insight. It can be compulsive and opportunistic. Victims may certainly be groomed, but the impulsive nature of the crime can put any child in the vicinity of a sex offender in danger. Many different psychological, biological, and sociological theories attempt to explain how and why deviant sexual preferences develop. Mental health professionals certainly attempt to develop intervention strategies that reduce repeat offending, but the prognosis for rehabilitating sex offenders is challenging. Rates of recidivism range from 18 percent to 45 percent (http://goo.gl/FKXOg).

The sad and tragic consequences of recidivism and predatory behavior can be seen in the case that changed the way in which sexually violent predators are incarcerated and treated in the state of California. On October 1, 1993, Richard Allen Davis climbed into a window in Petaluma, California, and abducted twelve-year-old Polly Klaas. Davis was on parole for a sex-related conviction on that ill-fated night. He sexually assaulted the child, strangled her to death, and left her body in a shallow grave. The fact that this offender had prior convictions outraged the public. There was an outcry for legislation that would better protect children and society from sexually violent offenders. In 1995, the California Legislature passed the Sexually Violent Predator Act (SVPA). This legislation permits the involuntary commitment of sexual offenders. The California

Welfare and Institution Code Section 6600(A) states a sexually violent predator is a person "who has been convicted of a sexually violent offense against one or more victims and who has a diagnosed mental disorder that makes the person a danger to the health and safety of others in that it is likely that he or she will engage in sexually violent criminal behavior." Currently, twenty states have civil commitment programs for sex offenders.

8.1 Part II: Surviving Abuse

Manifestation of psychological symptoms takes on a variety of expressions for the abused child. Though research has found that some children do not experience any changes in their psychological functioning, those who do are more likely to exhibit an increase in anxiety, sexually inappropriate behaviors, post-traumatic stress disorder symptoms, and depression (Cohen and Mannarino 1997; Brier 1992). Research has also found that parental support plays a significant role in the psychological recovery of the child (Cohen and Mannarino 1997). In a study focusing on treatment outcomes for sexually abused children, Cohn and Mannarino (1997) uncovered that parents who possessed strong coping skills and exhibited less distress could help their child to manage the effects of the abuse. They also recommended that parents "maintain normal rules and routines, as a way of reassuring that he or she is still the same child (i.e., not damaged) as before the sexual abuse occurred." In terms of treatment approaches, they found that a cognitive behavioral therapeutic frame and educating parents on the critical importance of providing support to their victimized child was the most beneficial intervention strategy.

There are times when research supports commonsense approaches to parenting. If your child has been victimized, showing support, love, and compassion is essential. Children need to know that their parents can handle even the most challenging crisis and that they have the strength to offer them help. In terms of treatment options, it becomes important to find a mental health professional who specializes in the treatment of sexually abused children. Ask questions regarding his\her training and background. Ask for the names of other parents who have used his\her services for the treatment of their own children. Support groups for parents of sexually abused children may offer a safe place in which to share your concerns and questions. Again, we focus on empowerment through knowledge, and the expansion of a skill set that is strong enough to address life's most challenging situations.

Another aspect of underage sexual intercourse that increases concern is our society's growing "normalization" of the practice. There are those organizations, such as the North American Man/Boy Love Association (NAMBLA), which suggest that it is normal and natural for adults to be attracted to children. Furthermore, they argue that the child is not harmed. NAMBLA and other pro-intergenerational relationship groups often state that there is no scientific evidence of harm. They claim that as society progresses, we will see the error of our ways. They argue that intergenerational sexual intercourse is not about sex but about love and an expression of that love. We reject these thoughts, ideas, and statements as absurd, dishonest, and destructive. Coercive sex is never about love but almost always about power, violence, or control. Children do not have the psychological or cognitive capacity to consent to a sexual relationship with an adult.

Several concepts discussed in this chapter should be implemented and used as a guide when making decisions regarding safety and decreasing the risk of victimization.

1. A very real and vital difference exists between healthy denial and purposeful indifference. As a parent, you need to make every possible effort to ensure the safety of your child (and then have trust and faith in those strategies) versus simply hoping that "nothing bad will happen to my child." Parents cannot blindly rely on other people's good nature.

81

A thorough risk assessment includes getting as much history as possible on those individuals in charge of watching your children. Use the Internet, talk to other parents, and ask for references. You need to gather data from multiple sources to uncover useable information. You must first be as sure as you can reasonably be of others' intentions and good nature before you allow them to be responsible for your kids.

2. Sex offenders prey on the innocent because many children and teens lack the skills that it takes to understand and interpret manipulative behavior exhibited by adults (especially when they know the assailant).

3. By understanding that sex offenders are not easily identifiable, we can avoid being manipulated because of a faulty assumption that a person poses no risk because he has money, is well dressed, appears intelligent, or doesn't look like someone who is attracted to children. If we assume that risk comes in all shapes and sizes, we are less likely to fall victim to a charismatic offender who is looking for a way to victimize others.

4. You have to teach your children to be cautious.

5. Multiple research projects and studies continue to empha-

size and drive home the point that friends or family members are most likely to sexually assault children.

6. Victims may certainly be groomed, but the impulsive nature of sex crimes can put any child in danger if he/she is in the vicinity of a sexual predator.

7. Manifestation of psychological symptoms takes on a variety of expressions for the abused child. Though research has found that some children do not experience any changes in their psychological functioning, those who do are more likely to exhibit an increase in anxiety, sexually inappropriate behaviors, posttraumatic stress disorder symptoms, and depression (Cohen and Mannarino 1997; Brier 1992).

Chapter 9

Home Safety Vignette

On the fifth of June, 2002, an adolescent girl named Elizabeth was kidnapped from her home while her younger sister Mary watched in horror. The abductor, a delusional drifter, climbed through an unlocked window and carried this petrified child into the darkness. As soon as she felt it was safe, Mary rushed to tell her parents that Elizabeth had just been kidnapped. Her parents listened in disbelief as she shared her real-life nightmare with them. How could one of their daughters be abducted from the safety of their home? Weren't all the doors and windows locked? How could Elizabeth have been kidnapped while they slept? Initially, they thought that Mary was in the midst of a terrible nightmare and tried to comfort her and send her back to bed. However, Mary was insistent. It wasn't until they searched the house that they realized with overwhelming horror that Elizabeth was gone.

An immediate search was organized. Friends, family, and neighbors quickly began to scour the surrounding area. Flyers were printed and distributed, websites were established, and the media were used to blitz the airways with the story of Elizabeth's abduction. Unfortunately, Elizabeth was not immediately found, and interest in the case began to diminish. While her family did everything possible to maintain focus on the abduction, the rest of the country assumed that Elizabeth was dead and, therefore, stopped searching. Research on child abduction reports that in 76 percent of the missing children cases studied, the abducted child was dead within three hours of the kidnapping. In 88.5 percent of the cases, the child was dead within twenty-four hours (`http://goo.gl/xXhda`). Nevertheless, against all odds, Elizabeth's family never gave up hope.

Over the course of the next nine months, this brave girl traveled the country and endured significant brutality at the hands of her captors. This man and his wife held the delusional belief that Elizabeth was to be one of his many wives. Elizabeth was forced to wear disguises and was rarely allowed to speak. She was under the constant watchful eye of her captors with almost no means of escape. It is likely that Elizabeth was suffering from Stockholm syndrome. Stockholm syndrome affects hostages who, over time, begin to identify with their captors (Stockholm syndrome takes its name from the first documented case, which occurred in Stockholm, Sweden, during a bank robbery).

For Elizabeth, her continued health and safety were solely in the hands of her captors. Stockholm syndrome can begin to develop over the course of several hours. Elizabeth was with these criminals for nine months. It is hard to fathom that despite all the research on Stockholm syndrome, there are still individuals who criticize this young girl (and other kidnapped children who have been held captive) for not making every effort to escape. To this, we would argue that unless you were there suffering with Elizabeth, you could not possibly understand the impact that the psychological and physical torture had on her psyche. The reality is that Elizabeth was found safe, and her abductors caught and prosecuted. She survived, and for that we have nothing but the utmost admiration and respect for her.

Chapter 10

Home Safety

The story of Elizabeth Smart illustrates clearly that no family is immune to the horrors associated with child abduction. Even though we want to believe that our neighborhoods are safe, our homes are secure, and predators will be kept at bay, the reality of life can come crashing down if it is your child who has been abducted. Some critics state that the media and other outlets are creating a paranoid culture. If this paranoia causes people to be more aware of risk, then we welcome the shift in beliefs. Personal and home safety must be approached like all other topics in this book — systematically, with purposeful decision making.

You may read the opening vignette in this chapter and think, "Well, that wouldn't happen to me, because I would never allow a stranger into my home." If we take an honest look at our rituals and behaviors, it may become evident that some of our everyday routines put us at risk. Do you always look through the peephole in your door when someone is knocking, or do you just open it without knowing who's standing on the other side? Do you keep your front door closed and locked even on a hot and humid summer day? How accessible is your home to predators? Do you know all of your neighbors? Have you looked online (through Megan's Law websites) to see where the closest sex offender lives? Though our homes can never be as secure as Fort Knox, increasing our awareness regarding potential risk can only help in our mission to be as safe as possible.

Our quest for securing our home begins with a reminder that there are people in this world who have no sense of compassion and live only to have their most immediate needs met. Given the opportunity, these predators will make your child (or you, for that matter) their next prey. Crimes of convenience and impulsivity go hand in hand. Criminals will take advantage of every opening that presents itself. An unsecured house is just another possible score. Though many of these suggestions sound elementary (like making sure doors and windows are locked) and logical, so often we forget crucial principles that can act as tremendous deterrents. To drive this point home even further, let's look at another dreadful, shocking, and horrific criminal act.

Four college-aged adults were experiencing a typical southern California evening in San Diego. They were enjoying the best of what the city had to offer — a condo on the beach just steps from the boardwalk. Like most of us, it is easy to imagine that they felt safe and secure in their home, unaware that before the night's end, their lives were going to be altered forever. Through an unlocked door, four perpetrators walked into their condo and began to terrorize and rape these two young couples for almost an hour. It appeared that they took immense pleasure in their crimes and tortured their victims (psychologically and physically). As if their heinous acts weren't shocking enough, these criminals then robbed their victims. As these perpetrators walked from the crime scene, a vigilant police officer noticed their suspicious behavior. They were questioned and apprehended. Fortunately, they were successfully tried, convicted and incarcerated.

The very nature of this crime was so appalling that during the court proceedings, the victims were not even able to retell their stories without breaking down. One of the victims reported that the events of that fateful evening fundamentally altered who she was as a person and how she viewed humanity. As if her faith in others wasn't damaged enough, during the course of the trial, these men were often seen laughing and taunting their victims. Their behavior demonstrated their total lack of compassion. They continued to victimize even in the confines of a San Diego courtroom.

These convicts chose their victims because it was easy. They saw an opportunity to attack and did so with reckless abandon. No forced entry, no broken windows, just an unlocked door that was opened by the twisting of a doorknob. A night defined by rape, assault, mayhem, and torture could have been prevented with a locked deadbolt. This illustrates how important it is to stick to the basics when securing your home. It is not our intention to make parents paranoid. We are simply trying to impress on you that safety cannot be taken for granted.

A locked door does us no good if we just haphazardly open it and allow the person on the other side access into our home. If your door does not have a peephole, installing one can provide increased security. We also can't stress enough the importance of establishing rules with your kids in reference to the manner in which they answer the door. It is our recommendation that you establish a list of neighbors, friends, and family who are the only people allowed in when you are not home. We further recommend a password that must be recited by the visitor before heshe is allowed in. As we established in the chapter on avoiding victimization, we need to be keenly aware of who we trust to watch our kids. Once this list is established, challenge your kids by having someone who is not on the list come to the door (with you observing close by). See how your child responds. Does heshe follow the rules, or just open the door? If heshe opens the door and allows the person inside, this becomes a perfect learning opportunity. Discuss with your child why it is important not to allow someone whom heshe doesn't know into the house. Be age appropriate. With teenagers, you can give specific examples that explain the risk. You do not need to be overly graphic, but a healthy dose of reality can help to change behavior. This can include reviewing your local Megan's Law website with them to further illustrate that convicted sex offenders are living within the community (remember, kids think nothing bad will ever happen to them). Childhood is called the "age of innocence" for a reason. As a parent, it is your job to help them to learn and engage in safe behaviors.

This same technique can also be used for strangers who approach in cars. Even though, from a young age, kids are told to avoid talking to strangers, time and time again we hear horror stories about sex offenders using a benign ruse to lure a child into their vehicle. If you set up a scenario in which your child is asked to approach a car driven by a stranger (you should be observing from close by), you can obtain a firsthand look at how heshe responds. We need to teach children new skills by providing realistic opportunities in which they can learn from their mistakes. We know that lecturing does not produce the desired effect. Instead, we need to teach them by using real-life scenarios and then discussing how interactions can be done differently. Role playing as a family is another way to engage in reality-based training. Allow each family member to take on a different character and see the response that it generates. Just like any other skill, safety needs to be taught and practiced in an easy-to-understand format. Another helpful tool that can be implemented is the development of a safety plan for the family to follow. This can be accomplished by having the family work together in the creation of rules and expectations that address a variety of situations. All important numbers should be placed on a list (including the nonemergency number to your local police department). It should also spell out the family rules in regard to talking with strangers, opening doors, and how to respond to emergency situations. Remember, in order for your kids to be invested in the plan, you must develop it together.

We practice reality-based training in the hopes that we can increase our awareness regarding common methods that criminals use to gain access to our children or homes. These skills are not just for kids but can also help the adults in the house to take a more proactive role in securing the homestead. The following true story further illustrates this point.

Cary Stayner, a serial killer from the Yosemite Valley, sexually assaulted and brutally killed two adult women and two teenagers before he was eventually caught and convicted. Stayner was a handyman at the hotel where his first three victims were staying. Since being caught, Stayner has reported that he fantasized about killing women for thirty years. On a cold night in February, his desire to kill could no longer be repressed. Stayner used a common ruse to gain access into the hotel room in which this mother (age forty-two), daughter (age fifteen), and family friend (age sixteen) were staying. He tricked them into opening their hotel door by stating that he needed to fix something in their room. Once inside, he brandished a weapon, and so began his murderous plot. He also killed another woman before being captured. Hideous, heinous, and horrific does not even begin to describe the brutality of his crimes. In a jailhouse interview, Stayner reminded all within earshot about the depth of a psychopath's lack of empathy for his victims. His response to why he chose to kill these woman and girls was simple, yet extremely telling. He explained that they were "just in the wrong place at the wrong time."

If we are being honest with ourselves, we can easily think of times when we let our guard down with a person whom, on some intuitive level, we know we should not trust. Sometimes listening to our gut is the most important step in our safety plan. Therefore, we need to think about common ways that criminals manipulate and disguise their true intentions. Their deceitful ways get us to invite them into our homes (or in the case of Stayner, a hotel room). A good exercise to implement during your role-playing scenarios is discussing what type of ruses criminals use to make us open an otherwise perfectly secured door. Here are a few to get you started.

1. "There's been an accident. Please let me in so I can use your phone." This ruse can be addressed by simply staying calm and asking the potential perpetrator what kind of accident it was and where it occurred. Do not open the door, but respond by stating, "I'm not going to open the door, but I will call 911 immediately." This must be reiterated time and time again with your child. Do not open the door; just call 911. Remember, reality-based training and role playing will help to drive this point home.

2. "The cable (telephone, Internet connection, etc.) is out next door. I need to check your connections to make sure that your system is not causing the problem." This ruse is somewhat more sophisticated, because right off the bat

you (or your child) will want to help your neighbor to get his/her cable back on. The person on the other side may also be wearing a uniform or work-specific clothing. Again, safety starts by not opening the door. Teach your children to look outside the nearest window. Is there a cable truck on the street? For parents, if you are home alone with your kids, think to yourself, why would a person need access into your home to fix a problem next door? Keep your wits about you and begin to ask questions. "For whom do you work?" "Can you give me the number to your call center?" "What is the work order number?" All these questions will give you insight into the legitimacy of the individual's request. Ultimately, though, you want to make sure that your child will not (under any circumstances) open the door for that workman. Teach your children to call you immediately to inform you that a stranger is at the door. If for some reason you are not available, have them call a family friend or trusted neighbor. Safety is often a community event. We all need to lend a helping hand to deter perpetrators from victimizing those whom we love and hold dear.

3. "We are thinking of buying a home (or renting an apartment) in this neighborhood. Can we come inside to look around?" This is another trick designed to gain access into

your home. By now the theme should be clear. Anyone wanting to come into your house for any unexpected reason should not be allowed access. This should be a nonnegotiable rule in your house that every family member follows under all circumstances. Concerning home and personal safety, there is no such thing as overreacting.

4. "Let me help you bring that (groceries, large item, etc.) inside." Another ruse designed to make you believe that this person has good intentions and is harmless. "What possible danger is there? This person is offering to help me." Again, the concept remains the same. With the exception of a workman who you have a scheduled appointment with and who can show identification, do not let strangers into your home.

Sticking to the basics in regard to physical safety also brings us to another fundamental component aimed at decreasing risk. The benefit of stressing physical fitness with your children is imperative. We need to be realistic. If a large adult confronts your child, his/her best option is to turn and run as fast as he/she possibly can. If he/she has already been grabbed, he/she must be taught to fight back. This includes screaming as loudly as possible that he/she is being kidnapped. Nothing is off limits. Biting, kicking, clawing, striking, and scratching any vital body part (the eyes, throat, and groin are always good targets) is imperative. Teaching your children to run toward safety (a neighbor's house, a crowded store) may be their last line of defense in an abduction scenario.

If your child is unable to run because of limited exercise or obesity issues, this may be the motivation that the family needs to address this potentially deadly lifestyle. Second, research continues to emphasize that depression and anxiety symptoms can be significantly decreased by engaging in an exercise program. The video game and technology culture has pulled kids off the kickball field and placed them in front of a television in their living room. Limited physical activity directly correlates with the expanding waistlines of today's youth. Many sex offenders are trawling the Internet and gaming sites right at this moment looking for vulnerable children and teens.

Self-defense classes for kids can also be an excellent way to develop a physical activity that helps them to stay safe and physically fit. From small towns to large metropolitan areas, numerous classes are available that focus on self-defense for kids and adolescents. You can certainly use your local police department or their community outreach officer for recommended classes or schools. If financial concerns are an issue, many programs offer one-day training where kids can learn the basics of self-defense. We would recommend that you attend with your child so that you can continue to practice after the class ends. Like any other skill, self-defense must be learned through practice and repetition.

Safety must be approached from all angles. It takes mental fortitude, physical strength (or at least a healthy fitness level), and awareness of our surroundings to uncover any dangerous situations. Sometimes the basics and a logical approach to security can be the most effective tools for keeping our children out of harm's way. Role modeling smart behavior can help to prepare your child to handle any situation that can have dire consequences if not approached from a safety standpoint. So what does all of this mean for you, the parent? Several concepts discussed in this chapter should be implemented and used as a guide when making decisions regarding safety.

1. Develop a safety plan as a family.

2. Personal and home safety must be approached like all other topics in this book — systematically, with purposeful decision making.

3. Given the opportunity, the criminal will take advantage of every opening that presents itself. An unsecured house is just another possible score.

4. Though many of these suggestions sound elementary (like making sure doors and windows are locked) and logical, so often we forget fundamental principles that can act as tremendous deterrents.

5. In regard to the appropriate age to leave a child home alone, maturity and his/her ability to handle a potential crisis should be the guiding factors in your decision making.

6. We can't stress enough the importance of establishing rules in regard to the manner in which kids answer the door. It is our recommendation that you establish a list of neighbors, friends, and family who are the only people allowed into your house when you are not home. You can even have a password that must be recited by the visitor before he/she is allowed in.

7. If a large adult confronts your child, the best option is to teach him/her to turn and run as fast as possible to get away from the threat. Teaching him/her to run toward safety (a neighbor's house, a crowded store, etc.) may be the last line of defense in an abduction scenario.

8. If your child has already been grabbed, he/she must be taught to fight back. This includes screaming as loudly as possible that he/she is being kidnapped. Nothing is off

limits. Biting, kicking, clawing, striking, and scratching any vital body part (the eyes, throat, and groin are always good targets) is imperative.

9. Self-defense classes for kids can also be a great way to develop a physical activity that is grounded in reality-based training. From small towns to large metropolitan areas, numerous classes are available that focus on self-defense for kids and adolescents.

Chapter 11

Sex and the Modern American Teen

Hypersexuality has become a dominant part of the American culture. From an early age, children are bombarded with graphic sexual images. What is deemed appropriate by today's standards would have made most people's grandparents blush. Just standing in line at the checkout stand in a grocery store can alter what is considered a normal expression of sexuality. The reality is that many young starlets are better known for their sexual escapades than for their roles in movies or their ability to carry a tune. Leaked nude pictures or a recorded sexual interlude makes breaking headline news as the images are spread around the web faster than a bullet train racing through the Japanese countryside. Is it really surprising that many computer viruses are packaged in junk mail that claims to have the latest and most relevant star engaged in a sexual act? Avoidance of these images is next to impossible. From roadside billboards to magazine ads, sex is used to sell almost every conceivable good or service. Overt sexuality has influenced the maturation process. Because of this, parents need to take a proactive approach and implement effective communication strategies to develop healthy ways to talk to their children about sex.

Current research suggests that parents are waiting too long to discuss sex with their children. "When it comes to talking about sex, parents are a few paces behind their kids. Too often, the birds-and-the-bees conversation occurs after, not before, kids start experimenting sexually, possibly in risky ways" (http://goo.gl/kcQKG). Let's be honest, for any parent, discussing sex is challenging, anxiety provoking, and downright scary. Unfortunately, avoidance and denial are not options. The risks associated with teen sex are real and can be life altering. From teen pregnancy to sexually transmitted diseases, choices made during adolescence can easily change the course of a child's life. Current statistics are staggering when we consider the rate of infectious disease and the long-term consequences associated with unprotected sex. According to the Centers for Disease Control (CDC), 48 percent of all high school students surveyed in 2007 acknowledged that they were sexually active, and 15 percent had already had intercourse with four or more partners during their lifetime. In that same year, 39 percent of sexually active teens reported that they did not use a contraceptive (condom) during their most recent sexual encounter. These staggering statistics directly correlate with the increase in HIV rates in adolescents. In 2006, the CDC estimated that almost 5,300 young people ages thirteen to twenty-four were diagnosed with HIV/AIDS. This number represented 14 percent of all individuals diagnosed during that same year. Unprotected sex is also contributing to the increase in rates for adolescents contracting other sexually transmitted diseases (including syphilis, gonorrhea, herpes, and HPV). Of the nineteen million new cases of STD infections, almost half of the diagnosed individuals are between the ages of fifteen and twenty-four (http://goo.gl/wu1dE) Currently, one in four teenage girls (estimated to be around 3.2 million) has a sexually transmitted disease (Forhan et al. 2009). Talking to your kids about sex can be a life-saving intervention. The stakes are too high to avoid dialogue strictly because the subject is awkward, embarrassing, or difficult to discuss.

Prior to any conversation with your teen, it is imperative to have a well-defined position regarding his/her potential sexual activity. Specifically, as parents, having a clearly focused message is extremely important. Parents will have to make their own choices regarding the expectations that they have for their child. Remember the theme of this book is about education, empowerment, and decreasing risk. It is not our intention to persuade you in one way or another regarding the boundaries and expectations that you have for your child. Yet, we must be realistic regarding the consequences related to early sexual activity. The decisions that you make as a family must take into account all the risk factors and dangers associated with all types of sexual contact. An educated and well-thought-out approach makes a difficult conversation much more bearable and effective. Open and honest dialogue has to be the foundation of any conversation that occurs regarding sex.

Parenting does not occur in a vacuum. So many outside influences affect how teens relate to and interact within their social community. Establishing household expectations regarding sexual intercourse, or any sexual behavior, for that matter, will help to frame how you establish the dialogue with your child. For instance, for your family, what age is appropriate for dating? Does that age shift when we take different options into consideration, including group outings versus a one-on-one date? Is abstinence the goal? A consistent, clear, and coherent message can help to clarify some of the confusion that develops during the maturation process. It is imperative to take into account the age of your child. Age-appropriate interventions are crucial in order for the conversation to be constructive and informative. How you address an eleven-year-old will differ from the conversation that you have with a sixteen-year-old. It must be reiterated that parents are waiting too long to discuss sex with their kids. Part of this problem stems from the fact that most conversations regarding sexual intercourse happen in a singular fashion or at best infrequently. Instead of seeing this as a topic that you discuss once, a more healthy and beneficial approach is to have ongoing dialogue. This will make it less taboo and also establish a healthy baseline for your kids to realize that they can talk to you about any subject. Research has shown that delayed onset of sexual activity for both boys and girls occurs when they have healthy and satisfying relationships with their parents (Caputo 2009).

One of the most valuable ways to develop a more effective approach to a difficult or challenging conversation is by implementing role playing into your repertoire of effective communication strategies. Role playing with your spouse or a trusted family member/friend can help you to develop the particular way in which you want to address this challenging topic. By practicing with another person, you will be able to lay out the specific aspects of the conversation that you believe are most relevant and significant. It will also help you to recognize the emotions that you will experience during the conversation. You want to have this exchange in the most rational and articulate manner. Discussing sex and sexuality with your child is anxiety provoking. Making sure that your own emotions do not skew your ability to effectively communicate becomes extremely important. If you are experiencing anxiety or difficulty discussing this subject, it is entirely appropriate to acknowledge this to your child. Healthy expression of emotion is good modeling. Remember that your children have spent their entire lives learning how to react to your emotions. Try to anticipate your child's response to questioning during the role play. Remember, lecturing is ineffective. Creating an environment in which your child feels comfortable and safe discussing an embarrassing topic with his/her parents is crucial. Dialogue about sex has to be fluid and flexible. It needs to be an ongoing conversation strictly because pressure to engage in all sorts of sexual behavior occurs throughout adolescence.

Here is a list of topics that will help to generate dialogue. The consequences associated with sexual behaviors have to be at the forefront of the conversation. Even if abstinence is the goal, you must still discuss the serious costs that can be associated with unprotected sex. Though this may feel like you are sending a mixed message, denial or complete faith that your child will remain abstinent can leave him unprepared regarding the real and present dangers associated with sexual intercourse. Even though teens often tune out hard facts and statistics, helping them to comprehend the risks associated with sex is essential. A simple intervention can be to search the web together for current infectious disease rates. The Centers for Disease Control website (http://www.cdc.gov) is an excellent place to start. Generating healthy dialogue begins by being open minded and allowing your child to express his/her views regarding sex. If your children are initially uncomfortable with this topic, ask them specific questions to help to generate dialogue. Talk to them about their views on abortion. What do they think about teen pregnancy? Are they aware of any classmates who are HIV positive or have another sexually transmitted disease? Remember, open-ended questions will generate healthy discourse. Specifically ask them how they feel, what they have experienced, and what kinds of problems they have faced. Do they think that they are emotionally ready to be in a sexual relationship? What are the consequences associated with engaging in sex with a boyfriend/girlfriend who then ends the relationship? These are very real issues and challenges that your kids will face through-out their adolescence. Like any other challenge in life, the more we tackle an obstacle, the easier it is to deal with. It is also im-portant to recognize the emotional component of your children's views on sex. By giving them the chance to acknowledge their confusion or concerns, it opens up the opportunity for them to explore their own thoughts, feelings, and even misconceptions about sex.

So much of what we have discussed up until this point in-cludes developing a proactive parenting style that confronts many obstacles and challenges that face the modern American teenager. A fundamental component of this interactive parenting model includes helping your child to develop a positive self-image and strong self-esteem. When you show faith in your kids and teach them how to make good and appropriate choices, they have tremendous control over the direction that their lives take. By implementing active listening skills, by parenting from a place of support and love, and by holding them accountable for their decisions, you help them to understand the link between choices and outcomes. Uncovering the link between healthy choices and behavior can be extremely enlightening. The teenage mind lives so much in the present that every skin blemish or social misstep can feel like the world is crashing all around him/her. Teaching your teenagers to be forward thinking and future oriented can help them to see past their social circle, which is so often defined by teenage angst. Empowerment includes teaching your children that they ultimately have control over their own bodies. Becoming infected with a sexually transmitted disease can be a lifelong consequence stemming from a single lapse in judgment. By emphasizing that their ideas and feelings are relevant and that their choices and decisions count, you provide a strong foundation for them to have the inner strength to avoid peer pressure. The more comfortable your child is in his own skin, the more likely he is to make good decisions. Help your children to see their potential by providing encouragement, support, love, and good role modeling. Be mindful of the messages you send. You can instill value and self-worth in your children by simply believing in their ability to make good decisions.

Sharing facts, statistics, and the real-life consequences associated with sexual contact does not have to be wrapped in dread. Fear-based interventions are short lived and are largely ineffective. Stressing abstinence or even safe sex practices does not have to become a power struggle if you focus on teaching, listening, and actively engaging with your teen. An approach that is based on fear and punishment often causes the opposite reaction and can certainly lead to a rift between parent and child.

Punishment does not teach your kids to avoid the behavior; instead, it teaches them to not get caught. If your own anxiety gets in the way of healthy dialogue, learn ways to decrease your stress and worry. When fear drives the intervention strategy, you will limit your effectiveness. Fear does not curb behavior; it only enhances poor decision making and shuts down effective communication.

Technology is contributing to degrading sexual experiences through inappropriate behaviors such as "sexting." In a nutshell, sexting is sharing sexually graphic images through the use of cell phones or social networking sites. Try to imagine the impact on your child's life if naked pictures were circulated throughout his/her school. Sexually fueled gossip (corroborated by pictures) can wreak havoc on a teen's sense of self and well-being. One single lapse in judgment can change the course of one's life. Another significant consequence linked to sexting is that transferring images of underage teens is a felony. Consider this: if a naked picture of a young girl is shared via cell phone with the majority of the student body, how many kids are breaking the law by forwarding those pictures? This is a very real problem with serious emotional and legal consequences. Sexting can become an alternate way to peddle child pornography.

Specific themes have been identified in research that analyzes teen behavior and abstinence. A review of the literature suggests that "involvement in religious activities and having positive peer role models appear to be protective factors related to delayed sexual intercourse amongst teens aged thirteen to fourteen years-old" (Doss et al. 2006). Families who attend religious services raise teens who are less likely to become sexually active at a young age. Studies suggest that abstinence and delayed onset of sexual activity occur in families in which parents have strong religious beliefs, attend religious services together, and participate in religious activities. These factors contribute to abstinence prior to the age of eighteen for both boys and girls (Caputo 2009). In regard to peer role models, deviant peer involvement was a robust predictor of early sexual activity (Caputo 2009). Intuitively, this makes perfect sense. If your child is spending time with friends who engage in destructive behaviors (i.e., smoking cigarettes, illicit drug use, drinking alcohol), his risk for acting out increases exponentially. In contrast, one of the most significant predictors of delayed sexual intercourse occurs with teens who are involved in a peer group whose members support abstinence. The National Campaign to Prevent Teen Pregnancy (2005) reported that teens who attend religious services regularly were more likely to remain abstinent. Peer support contributes to a collective move toward delayed sexual activity.

Positive peer role modeling and normalizing abstinence occurs amongst teens who participate in religious services together.

If you are comfortable with your child being sexually active, there must be a clear understanding that early sexual experiences have the potential to shape lifelong attitudes regarding sex (which can affect all future relationships). Developing healthy attitudes toward intercourse and stressing the importance of safe sex is imperative. To avoid degrading sexual experiences or victimization, your child needs to have a strong sense of who he/she is and respect for his/her body (and psychological well-being, for that matter). Though changing cultural expectations may normalize sexually acting out behaviors, this does not have to become acceptable within the walls of your home. The National Campaign to Prevent Teen Pregnancy reported that 81 percent of sexually active teenagers (between twelve and fourteen years old) wished that they had waited longer to engage in sexual activity. Adolescents who begin to engage in sexual intercourse at a young age are at increased risk for teen pregnancy and sexually transmitted diseases; they also have more sexual partners over time and are at a higher risk of becoming HIV positive (Doss et al. 2006). A parenting style that is supportive, loving, and engaging helps to decrease risk and contributes to a family dynamic that develops a strong sense of self and coping skills that aid in healthy decision making.

Several concepts discussed in this chapter should be implemented and used as a guide when discussing sexual activity and abstinence.

1. Current research suggests that parents are waiting too long to discuss sex with their children.

2. The risks associated with teen sex are real and can be life altering. From teen pregnancy to sexually transmitted diseases, choices made during adolescence can easily change the course of a child's life.

3. Prior to any conversation with your teen, it is imperative to have a well-defined position regarding his/her potential sexual activity. Specifically, as parents, having a clearly focused message is extremely important. Age-appropriate interventions are crucial in order for the conversation to be constructive and informative.

4. Role playing with your spouse or a trusted family member/friend can help you to develop the particular way in which you want to address this challenging topic. By practicing with another person, you will be able to lay out the specific aspects of the conversation that you believe are the most relevant and significant.

5. A fundamental component of this interactive parenting model includes helping your child to develop a positive self-image and strong self-esteem. When you show faith in your kids and teach them how to make good and appropriate choices, they have tremendous control over the direction that their lives take.

6. By implementing active listening skills, by parenting from a place of support and love, and by holding them accountable for their decisions, you help them to understand the link between choices and outcomes.

7. Fear-based interventions are short lived and are largely ineffective. Stressing abstinence or even safe sex practices does not have to become a power struggle if you focus on teaching, listening, and actively engaging with your teen.

8. Studies suggest that abstinence and delayed onset of sexual activity occur in families in which parents have strong religious beliefs, attend religious services together, and participate in religious activities.

Chapter 12

Drugs and Alcohol Vignette

Drug intoxication can have severe and significant consequences, even for first-time or recreational users. While working as an on-call psychologist in a local ER, a couple brought their daughter into the hospital because she was "acting bizarre." Over the course of the next several hours, this eighteen-year-old girl experienced her first psychotic break, which included auditory and visual hallucinations, disorganized thinking, and bizarre delusions that caused her to yell, scream, and become so violent that she had to be physically restrained. Her parents, clearly and understandably distraught, wanted to know what could cause this kind of deterioration in her psychological stability. An evaluation of her urine drug screen gave the answer. She was positive for amphetamine use.

Initially, her parents thought that the test was inaccurate or at least a false positive. They were in denial regarding their daughter's drug use and stated repeatedly, "She doesn't use drugs. Maybe the test is wrong? She was taking cough medicine, could that be it?" It was certainly understandable that this news came as a shock; however, it was much more important for them to accept the results of the urine analysis and to help to get their daughter into an appropriate treatment setting. It was also stressed to them that it was detrimental and dangerous to ignore the fact that their little girl was clearly abusing stimulants. Most disconcerting to her parents at the time was her psychotic behavior. They asked, "Can drugs really do that to a person? She is so young; doesn't a person have to be using for years and years to act like this? When will she be better?" They were told that drugs can make a person psychotic and that the list of intoxicants that can cause a psychiatric episode includes not only methamphetamine but also cocaine, ecstasy, and even legal synthetic drugs. A person does not have to be a lifelong user for drugs to have this kind of effect. Substance-induced psychosis can occur after a single use.

Her parents were told that their daughter was going to be admitted to a psychiatric facility for her own safety. They were informed that in the best-case scenario, the psychotic symptoms would dissipate as the intoxication wore off. If she remained a danger to herself or others, the hospital would keep her on a psychiatric hold until she became stable. They were also told that regardless of what happened in the morning, it was imperative to help her to get into a substance abuse treatment program.

The next morning, this young woman had, in fact, gotten better and was no longer experiencing the hallucinations or delusions that had plagued her the night before. Upon her discharge, the doctors again stressed the importance of treatment. They also told the woman and her parents that stimulant abuse can cause permanent brain abnormalities and dysfunction.

Roughly two weeks later, the police again brought this young woman back into the Emergency Room after she was exhibiting many of the same psychotic behaviors. When her parents got to the ER, they had the same looks of concern and disbelief. When asked by the responding hospital staff, "What happened?" they responded, "Well, we decided to take her to New York City. We wanted to reward her for graduating from high school. We planned on putting her in a program after we got back."

Unfortunately this story does not have a Hollywood ending. This young woman did not recover from her overdose. She continued to experience severe psychotic symptomology even after the initial intoxication wore off. Her drug use altered her brain functioning and caused significant long-term psychological and social impairment. The sad reality is that this story plays out over and over again in ERs throughout this country. The drug epidemic is a worldwide problem that continues to create chaos and leave destruction and death in its wake.

Chapter 13

Addiction

Helping your child to develop insight into the importance of healthy decision making has been a core component of this book. Illicit drug use and alcohol consumption are aspects of life that the dominant culture reinforces. Intoxication is revered and almost expected as a rite of passage. Addiction and physiological damage to the brain and body are often left out of this glorified version of fun. We have already established that the adolescent brain is geared toward impaired decision making. Between the "imaginary audience," limited life experiences, and the difficulty comprehending that choices today can have lifelong consequences, surviving adolescence is challenging enough without compromised judgment. If we think back on our own adolescence, most of us can easily conjure up experiences or decisions that still make us cringe. This partly explains why parents are so anxious about their teen's safety and decision-making ability. Mixing drugs and alcohol with an already diminished capacity for healthy choices can easily become a serious recipe for disaster. Your children will, at some point, be offered drugs or alcohol. It is a reality that all parents must accept. This is why it is so imperative to discuss this topic with your teen before the grips of addiction are tearing at the very fabric of your family. Your job as a parent is to discuss with your teens the realities of drug abuse, the multitude of consequences associated with addiction, and how rapidly life can spiral out of control when behaviors are fueled by drug and alcohol consumption. Just like the conversations regarding sexual behavior, this topic needs to be discussed early and often. Age-appropriate conversation can begin as early as elementary school.

Parents often have questions about the origins of addiction. How does a person become addicted in the first place? Why can't he/she simply quit? Is it truly a disease or just lack of willpower? These questions are complex, and many theorists have conducted research in an effort to answer these same questions. In order to address addiction, it is important for parents to have a fundamental understanding of the research that discusses this very pertinent topic. When a family is struggling with a loved one who is in the throes of addiction, time and energy are often spent blaming or looking to blame some outside force or person. This time and energy could be better spent supporting and assisting the addict. An appropriate understanding of addiction will also assist the family to select the most effective and appropriate treatment options. Several leading theories attempt to explain the origins of addiction. Our main goal for this chapter is to integrate theory with practical applications and intervention strategies. Human beings have struggled with addiction for thousands of years. Archeologists report that early Sumerians had an ideogram for opiate use (Lindesmith 1968), and the earliest historical record of alcohol production was a brewery mentioned in an Egyptian papyrus in 3500 BC (Fort 1971). In 2000 BC, an Egyptian priest preached prohibitionist teachings in his theological writings. He stated, "I, thy superior, forbid thee to go to the taverns. Thou art degraded like beasts" (Crafts and Leitsch 1909). Clearly, substance abuse and addiction are not new issues.

Some of the earliest thoughts and ideas about addiction were centered on what is called "the moral theory." The moral theory of addiction states that people who become addicts generally do so because of some spiritual flaw, lack of willpower, or other character defect. According to the moral theory, if addicts simply tried harder, had more faith, or were more devout in prayer, they would be able to overcome their addiction. They are seen simply as weak. The moral theory also holds that addicts simply choose to abuse drugs and alcohol. Although it is clear that there is some element of choice in all human behavior, it would be a mistake to minimize the psychological, biological, and social factors that contribute to addiction. As our understanding of anatomy, physiology, genetics, sociology, and psychology has expanded, we have seen that the moral theory simply does not explain all the different facets of addiction. Research shows that there is power in prayer, and we firmly believe in incorporating faith-based treatment interventions for those individuals who find them efficacious. However, the moral theory of addiction often does more harm than good. When family members see addiction only from this perspective, they often become angry and frustrated by the addict's behavior. This limits intervention strategies simply because this theoretical frame states that the only reason for addiction is personal choice and weakness of character.

Another popular theory of addiction is called the genetic theory. The genetic theory of addiction holds that addicts are genetically predisposed to substance abuse and dependency. In other words, if Jim has a drink and becomes an addict and Tom does not, it is because there is something in Jim's genetic coding that predisposes him to be more susceptible to alcohol. Jim was going to be an alcoholic regardless of parenting, early environmental factors, and so forth. One of the more common arguments in support of the genetic theory comes from what we know about the children of addicts. Research has shown that sons of alcoholic fathers are four times more likely to develop alcoholism than sons of nonalcoholic fathers (Woodside 1988).

Genetic theorists attempt to separate environmental causes from genetic causes. This is often done through research on children who are genetically predisposed to addiction but were adopted into families where neither parent struggled with substance abuse. The research suggests that children who come from addicted families are more likely to develop dependency than those who are not genetically predisposed (Woodside 1988). Though the research seems to suggest a genetic link, environmental causes can also impact addiction. It is difficult to isolate genetics as the primary cause of increased addiction levels with adopted children simply because a host of psychological and social influences could have affected their level of risk and exposure. For example, if a child grows up in an environment in which addiction is present and the primary caregiver is engaging in self-destructive behavior, it is more likely that the dysfunctional environment will negatively impact this child's psychological stability. Stress and chaos in early childhood are also strongly linked to addiction. Given that this is the case, however, how do we tease out what part of the addictive behavior is genetic and what part is a result of growing up in a chaotic and dysfunctional household?

Closely related to the genetic theories are the biological theories of addiction. These theories attempt to account for different anatomical and physiological factors that contribute to addictive behavior (including brain chemistry, the size of different neurological structures, etc.). Some of the research, for example, suggests that addicts' brains respond differently when provided with images of alcohol or drugs. Magnetic resonance imaging (MRI) studies show that the addict's brain "lights up" when he/she is exposed to these pictures. Other brain imaging studies show how the brain structures of addicts differ significantly from those of nonaddicts. The advancements made in neuroimaging have provided tremendous insight into how the brain responds to drugs and alcohol, and the physiological changes that occur due to addiction. Addiction alters brain functioning by disrupting the "reward centers" of the brain. Cocaine, for example, vastly increases the availability of dopamine in the synapses of the brain's neurons. This creates the sense of euphoria that cocaine users crave. It also explains why prolonged cocaine use often leads to psychosis, because elevated dopamine levels are also associated with psychotic symptoms. The scientific community continues to debate about whether the changes that we see in the biology of addicts are a cause of addiction or an effect of addiction. Unfortunately, it is very difficult to conduct research on addicts prior to their addiction. This limits the ability of researchers to compare and contrast brain imaging pre- and post-addiction. Therefore, researchers do not know if the difference in brain anatomy and physiology are due to prolonged chemical use or if those differences existed prior to exposure to illicit substances. Another major criticism of this model has to do with the role of choice in addiction. Differing brain structures and brain chemistry do not necessarily mean that a person has no choice regarding his behavior, including whether or not to use. This is a very important concept because for every addict who hopes to get clean, there must be the desire to implement behavioral change. Examples include the choice to go to rehab, the choice to avoid using, the choice to take responsibility for his/her addiction, and so forth.

The final concept is called the psychological theory. This theory postulates that addiction is a function of psychological pain. If an individual is sufficiently anxious, depressed, or experiencing emotional distress, he/she is more likely to turn to mind-altering substances to ease that pain. This can quickly initiate a downward cycle into addiction. Another phrase that is often used to describe this phenomenon is self-medicating. Instead of finding help or learning new coping skills, people who are prone to addiction turn toward drugs and alcohol. This is a quick and very short-sighted approach to life's difficulties. Addicts can often be heard making comments such as, "You have no idea how much I love crystal (methamphetamine)." They will discuss their drug of choice as if they are talking about their best friend; always there to soothe, always understanding, and never judgmental. This is in direct contrast to most other people in their lives. Others are seen as always nagging, harping on them to get clean, threatening, or mistreating them in some way or manner. Another way to conceptualize this theory is to think of addiction as a symptom of a greater problem; a symptom of misery, for example. If the misery can be treated or resolved, it is much more likely that the addiction can be successfully addressed. This also explains why so many people trade addictions. An alcohol addiction can quickly become a cocaine, marijuana, or heroin addiction because they all do the same thing — ease psychological pain. The marijuana addict can seamlessly trade marijuana for pornography, sex, or gambling because the desired effect does not change between addictions.

Of the different theories of addiction, the psychological theory best accounts for choice. This theory places the onus of recovery on the addict, empowering him with the ability to stop. Criticisms of this theory include its inability to address the genetic component of addiction. The psychological theory also often gets confused with the moral theory. To be clear, the psychological theory does not say that an addict needs to choose his way out of addiction; it simply says that choice is involved and plays the most significant role in recovery. Finally, the psychological theory views the origins of most, if not all, addictions as the same. From this perspective, there is little significant difference between alcohol dependence and a gambling addiction. The only noteworthy differences between addictions are the effects that they have on the body, a function of the biological theory. This is an important distinction, however, because those differences do account for the variance that we see in the success rates of sobriety compared across substances. For example, the physiological effects of heroin are much more powerful than the physiological effects of marijuana.

It is clear from the research in the field of chemical dependency that the reality of addiction and its origin is that all of the above theories are in play. Clear anatomical and physiological consequences have been established in neuroimaging and may even be present and a precursor to addiction. Genetics and environmental influences further complicate the picture. Ultimately, human beings are complex creatures whose emotional framework and processing cannot be discounted when treating addiction.

Brain development plays a crucial role in our psychosocial functioning. The use of drugs and alcohol during adolescence can have an adverse effect on the rapidly developing teenage brain. A malfunctioning brain can alter the way in which we engage with others socially, psychologically, and behaviorally. Several studies have suggested that heavy teenage alcohol use appears to be linked to long-term problems with memory function, attention, visuospatial skills, planning, abstract reasoning, and goal-directed behavior (http://goo.gl/F3rqZ). Developing brain structures altered by illicit drugs can cause significant behavioral change. It is important to recognize that during adolescence, "Millions of new synapses (connections between brain cells) in the frontal lobe are created and organized. Nerve cells develop a fatty coating called myelin during adolescence, which allows the brain to function more efficiently" (Watkins et al. 2006, p. 131). During this stage of brain development, research has shown that teens are more at risk of addiction due to their biological vulnerability (Watkins et al. 2006). For most adult addicts, their introduction to drugs and alcohol began during adolescence.

From a structural standpoint, the continuing development of the frontal lobe during adolescence is one of the most significant components of brain development. The frontal lobe (composed of a large region of the neocortex) is the part of the brain that is responsible for voluntary movement, impulse control, memory, speech production, and decision making (White 2003). The physiological changes that occur within the frontal lobe during adolescence enable the adult brain to function properly. Research suggests that disruption during the development of the frontal lobe can have long-term consequences, "which raises the possibility that drug abuse could alter the normal development of the frontal lobe during adolescence either by directly affecting the brain or by simply depriving the individual of normal, healthy interactions with the environment" (White 2003, p. 40). Because of the increased vulnerability of the brain, intervention strategies based on abstinence and education are vital.

The hippocampus is another area of the brain that is affected by the consumption of alcohol during adolescence. This part of the brain is primarily involved in the formation of new memories and learning. Current research suggests that alcohol use by adolescents damages this crucial structure of the brain by causing the hippocampus to shrink. This alters brain functioning by creating impairment in both memory and learning. "Heavy-drinking patterns in adolescents and young adults are linked to smaller hippocampi and, because these brain structures are critical to learning and memory formation, may lead to more severe impairment of memory function" (Tapert 2004, p. 208). Both the neocortex and the hippocampus are in a sense establishing the hardwiring of the brain, which is going to affect cognitive functioning throughout adulthood. The adolescent brain is physically changing by the creation of neuropathways that develop through new experiences and interactions with the outside world. "Neuroplasticity refers to the ability of circuitry in the brain to physically change and grow new dendrites as a result of new learning and experience" (`http://goo.gl/hm5jc`). Alcohol and drugs disrupt this development, which can alter and influence a person's behavior and personality for the rest of his/her life.

Because the teenage brain is more susceptible to addiction, helping your child to manage this precarious time is absolutely critical. When it comes to drugs and alcohol, parents must take an active role in confronting any substance abuse that is occurring. Fear and denial become a parent's biggest enemy. It is too easy to discount drug and alcohol use as "experimentation" or a "rite of passage"; yet, this perspective can lead to complacency or flat-out denial. Parenting includes holding your children accountable for any risky behavior. If you suspect that your teenager is using (even on an occasional basis), it is imperative that you begin an open and honest dialogue regarding his substance use. Too many parents make the mistake of not addressing this issue when it initially occurs. If not confronted, experimentation can easily turn to addiction. Parents can enable at-risk behavior by not addressing the risks associated with drugs and alcohol. The inactive parent enables drug use. By turning a blind eye, the risk of addiction increases exponentially. The more involved you are, the greater protection you provide to your child.

Another aspect of teens' susceptibility to addiction is influenced by limited coping skills. The cultural challenges associated with growing up in America have been discussed numerous times within this book. It is important to remember that developmentally, teenage angst is significantly influenced by a lack of coping skills. As adolescents mature into adulthood, they learn new ways to combat stress, anxiety, and social pressures. During adolescence, many of these skills are just beginning to be learned (usually through trial and error) and implemented. Another contributing factor of addiction is influenced by this lack of coping skills. If a teen is struggling with an issue and can use alcohol, for instance, as a way to manage his/her fear, anxiety, or depression, he/she learns (and reinforces) that all that is needed to tackle life's problems is a mind-altering substance. "Comorbidity" is a term psychologists use to describe the existence of two disorders. The adolescent who is self-medicating to address an underlying psychological issue can easily travel the road toward addiction. This is why it is so important to be hyperaware regarding how your child is interacting with you, his/her friends, and other family members. If you notice a significant change in behavior, talk to your teen and try to uncover what is causing the change in psychological functioning. Is he/she depressed? Is he/she being targeted by a bully at school? Is he/she using drugs or alcohol? Just like a good detective, parents need to uncover any evidence that may be contributing to an altered mood state.

Numerous studies have shown that an active parenting style decreases the likelihood that your child will abuse alcohol and drugs. When we consider the risks associated with substance abuse — including increased risk of death or injury from motor vehicle accidents, mental health problems including suicide, risky sexual behavior, sexual assault, decreased brain functioning, and, of course, lifelong addiction — the more active a role a parent plays, the better the outcome. "Studies have consistently demonstrated that effective parenting practices have a strong impact on reducing the risk of early alcohol consumption. Different facets of effective parenting have all been shown to be important, including parental monitoring and supervision, expression of unambiguous disapproval of underage drinking, and low levels of parent-child hostility" (Aria 2007).

There are times when research supports a logical approach to parenting. The first component of decreased risk includes monitoring and supervising your children. This includes knowing specifically who their friends are and how they are spending their time socially. If you turn a blind eye to at-risk behavior, your child will see this as a free pass. Supervision and monitoring includes staying active and involved in your children's lives. Second, an active parenting style includes openly discussing your disapproval regarding underage drinking and substance abuse. If you set the expectation for your household to be drug and alcohol free, your teen is less likely to use. A study by Nash (2003) looked at the impact that parent disapproval had on underage drinking. Nash followed a group of high school freshmen for four years and monitored their drinking patterns throughout high school. They found that students whose parents disapproved of underage drinking had significantly lower rates of alcohol use compared to their peers whose parents took a more detached approach. The research also suggested that parental disapproval helped to mediate the influence of peer pressure on alcohol consumption (Nash 2003)

Effective communication and an active parenting style help to decrease conflict and reinforce a supportive home life. Low parent-child hostility is a protective factor simply because a decrease in turmoil and conflict creates a more open and loving environment. When children feel like they are supported, loved, and understood by their parents, they are more confident and secure. Parents can never underestimate the impact that they have on their child's development. Modeling healthy behavior and effective communication strategies will teach your children how to interact successfully with those around them. This helps them to improve their coping skills and self-confidence. Support and love help a child to develop a healthy self-image and the confidence to navigate this often confusing and difficult world.

If you suspect that your child is exhibiting signs and symptoms of excessive drug or alcohol use, action is absolutely necessary. It is also important to recognize that specific drugs gain and lose popularity due to accessibility and cost. Synthetic or "designer drugs" are often packaged as herbal products and are legal in most states. Though legal, these drugs can be just as damaging as traditional street drugs. This is a good reminder that the illegal and legal narcotic landscape is always changing. Addiction can be triggered by so many different substances. Do not hesitate to have a mental health professional (specifically one who specializes in addiction) conduct a thorough evaluation of your child. The severity of the chemical dependency often dictates the most effective and appropriate treatment option. It is important to become a student of recovery and to understand the primary frame for the addiction of treatment. Ask pertinent questions and advocate for your child. A better understanding of the process will allow parents to be informed consumers and help them to choose the most appropriate interventions for their teen. In the next several paragraphs, we will detail the steps most commonly followed between the stages of addiction and sobriety.

13.1   Interventions/Road to Recovery

Inpatient Detoxification: Inpatient detoxification refers to a process in which the patient is admitted to a hospital and given medicine that will allow him/her to "come off" the drugs or alcohol while minimizing the impact of the withdrawal symptoms. This process usually takes five to ten days. This is most commonly done for patients who have been using alcohol, heroin, pain pills, or antianxiety pills. The withdrawal symptoms associated with alcohol and antianxiety pills are potentially fatal. For this reason, a medically monitored detoxification process is almost always recommended. The withdrawal symptoms associated with cocaine, marijuana, ecstasy, and other drugs, while uncomfortable, are not potentially fatal. This is why a medically monitored detoxification process from those substances is not recommended, and there are very few, if any, insurance plans that pay for them.

If you believe that your teen is in need of inpatient detox, the simplest thing to do is to take him to your local emergency room. Bring any pills that you may find, and be prepared to give a thorough history of your teen's use. This, along with the physical examination and blood and urine tests that will be done in the emergency department, will assist the treating physician in determining whether inpatient detox is appropriate for your child. If it is deemed appropriate, your child will be admitted to the hospital, where a detox process can begin.

Inpatient Rehabilitation: Inpatient rehab is the step that most commonly follows inpatient detox. Outside of recovery circles, these two options are often mistakenly regarded as interchangeable. Detox is a process that is done in a hospital where the patient is closely monitored by medical staff; rehab is often done in a facility best described as a step down from a hospital. Most rehabilitation programs also include medications as part of their regimen, but these differ from the medications used in an acute detox process. Rehabilitation programs will often include components designed to address the physical, spiritual, social, and psychological well-being of the addict. The length of these programs can range anywhere from thirty to ninety days, and sometimes up to a year or more, depending on the severity of the addiction. These programs often begin with a very structured approach to recovery. As the addict moves through the program, he usually "earns" privileges that will sometimes include the ability to go out into the community and work. Inpatient rehabilitation may also include programs designed to help family members to understand their role in the addictive process.

The advantage of an inpatient rehabilitation program is that it has the addict as a "captive audience." At first, your teen will be allowed minimal contact with the outside world. During this time frame, he/she will be working to identify and change the self-destructive behaviors that led to the addiction. As he/she works through this process, he/she eventually transitions to a lifestyle that better mirrors the real world. The goal of inpatient rehabilitation is ultimately to help the addict to learn adaptive skills and strategies to cope with the stressors that likely contributed to the addiction.

Partial Hospitalization Program (PHP): A PHP is a program in which the addict is in a treatment setting that includes eight hours of treatment per day for five days a week. The difference between a PHP and inpatient rehab is that the former allows the patient to go home at night, and he does not attend the program on the weekends. This type of program will include group and individual therapy, family therapy, and medication review.

Intensive Outpatient Program (IOP): An IOP is a step down from a PHP. An IOP meets two to three times per week for three to four hours at a time. An IOP will include all of the elements of the PHP and rehab program with the understanding that, at this point, the patients have made significant improvement and strides in their functioning and understanding of their addiction. An addict is ready for this less-structured environment when he/she is able to live an addiction-free life with a lower level of care and supervision.

Twelve-Step Meetings: A significant feature of any addiction treatment program will include "twelve-step" meetings. A quick Internet search will reveal that there are twelve-step meetings for virtually every possible known addiction. The efficacy of twelve-step meetings is beyond the scope of this book, but one thing is certain people who attend twelve-step meetings swear by them, and virtually every addict with whom we have ever worked who has relapsed has the same answer to the question "What happened, why did you relapse?" They say, "I stopped going to meetings."

Finding the right level of treatment will take professional guidance. Advocate for the most appropriate setting and take an active role in your teen's recovery. Support, love, and good, healthy boundaries and expectations will help to break the grips of addiction. Most, if not all, programs offer treatment for family members as well. We recommend that you use this opportunity and take advantage of these programs in order to learn what role, if any, the family may have had in your teen's addictive process. This will further enhance the likelihood that he/she will continue to live his/her life addiction free.

Chapter 14

Adolescents and Mental Health

During any stage of development and growth, it is completely normal for children to express a wide range of emotions. Part of the maturation process includes learning how to articulate, react to, and feel the emotions that make us uniquely human. The normal expression of sadness, anger, mood fluctuations, and even happiness plays an important role in learning how to navigate this often challenging and frustrating world. Unfortunately, many of the serious mental illnesses that plague adults can begin to manifest and develop in children. The United States Department of Human Services estimates that at least one in five children and adolescents exhibits enough symptoms to be diagnosed with a mental health disorder; these include depression, attention deficit/hyperactivity, anxiety, conduct, and eating disorders. They also state that about one in ten children/adolescents experiences "serious emotional disturbances" that cause significant disruption in the way in which he/she interacts with his/her peers, participates in school, or engages with other members of his/her community (`http://goo.gl/ohCtu`).

Understanding the signs and symptoms of mental illness or mood disturbances is important and relevant because it can help you distinguish between behaviors that are a normal part of adolescent development and those that are of greater concern. If left untreated, mental health issues can prove to be extremely problematic. Psychological disturbances can lead to a significant change in functioning, including poor school performance, family conflict, sexually acting out behaviors, violence, and even suicide. A working base of knowledge regarding the signs and symptoms of mental illness will increase insight and understanding about this extremely important topic. This chapter will provide an overview of disorders so that you have the ability to make educated decisions about appropriate intervention strategies, including when professional help is needed. Remember, any dramatic change in functioning should be assessed by a medical or psychiatric professional. Certain medical conditions can exacerbate or mimic mental health issues. A thorough medical workup is always encouraged to uncover the root cause of any change in emotional functioning.

The causes of mental health issues are complex and open to much debate. The nature (biology/genetics) versus nurture (environment/family atmosphere) argument has been going on for decades. In reality, a multitude of influences impact and affect a child's development. The biological factors that can contribute to the onset of mental illness can include genetic abnormalities, chemical imbalances, and traumatic brain injuries (TBIs). TBIs can have a tremendous impact on the overall functioning of a child or adolescent by causing problems within the central nervous system, disrupting intellectual capabilities, and affecting judgment and reasoning (http://goo.gl/3w711). From a nurture standpoint, traumatic events, including physical and sexual abuse, can increase the risk of psychological disturbances. Violence, in its many forms (including child abuse, sexual assaults, witnessing spousal abuse, and gang violence), can also be a trigger for mental illness. Other stressors, including poverty, broken homes, and the loss of loved ones through divorce or death, can also contribute to and alter the psychological stability of a child (http://goo.gl/3w711).

Witnessing changes in a child's psychological functioning can be both frightening and overwhelming. Yet, the reality of adolescence brings with it a normal range of emotional turmoil and angst that most teenagers experience. For parents, one of the most helpful tools in understanding mental health issues can be having a working knowledge regarding the normal expression of symptoms versus those that are pathological. This chapter will take an in-depth look at depression, bipolar disorder, and ADHD. It will provide an overview of symptoms, intervention strategies, ways to advocate for your child, and resources that can help you and your family. Readily identifiable signs and symptoms of distress are important for parents to acknowledge and recognize. (We have decided not to cover anxiety specifically in this chapter because most of the research on anxiety suggests that it is often a comorbid diagnosis. This means that if your child is expressing significant anxiety, he may be experiencing some level of depression or other mood disorder that warrants treatment. Treating the comorbid illness can result in an alleviation or decrease in anxiety symptoms.)

When discussing behavior in children and adolescents, it is always important to remember context. As a parent, more than any other person, you should be familiar with your child's moods and behavior. Though teachers, doctors, family members, and others can provide good collateral information regarding your teen's behavior, the reality is that you should be constantly assessing your child's emotional presentation. This is especially true if he is distressed or exhibiting behaviors that are out of the ordinary. In reality, the establishment of a baseline for behavior becomes one of the most important parental assessment techniques. When you have a solid understanding of their usual behavioral patterns as well as the context for their behavior, it becomes easier for you to identify changes that are potentially worrisome. For starters, let us look at the symptoms that are present in clinical depression. Discussing depression is important because at its most severe, it can cause suicidal ideation and lethal behaviors. Suicide research and statistics report that the risk of suicide increases as children age and enter adolescence. According to the CDC, suicide is the third leading cause of death for fifteen to twenty four year olds. Suicide is only surpassed by car accidents and homicide. It is impractical to think that a teenager is never going to exhibit signs of sadness or melancholy. Mood swings are a normal part of adolescent development; but when the impairment becomes severe, clinical depression may be evident. This is why developing a baseline for your children's behavior is so important. If they are acting differently for an extended period, or if you notice a significant change in functioning in school, during family outings, or while they are interacting with their peers, you may want to consider having them assessed for depression. Specifically, depressive symptoms in teens often manifest with a significant increase in irritability and agitation. This expression of symptoms can include angry outbursts and a low frustration tolerance. Teenagers struggling with depression may also complain about physical ailments, including stomach pains and headaches. The physical manifestation of depressive symptoms in teens can make it more difficult to uncover the root cause, but after being cleared medically, you may want to consider depression as a possibility if the problems persist. Along with these symptoms, depression in teenagers may also include an increase in sadness and feelings of hopelessness, changes in sleep patterns, difficulty concentrating, loss of appetite, feelings of worthlessness, low self-esteem, and suicidal ideation (American Psychiatric Association [DSM-IV-TR] 2000). Collateral contact from teachers, family members, or friends can provide valuable information regarding their mood state. Depression is pervasive and can cause impairment in almost all aspects of your child's life.

When we consider that teenage suicide is the third leading cause of death for the fifteen-to-twenty-four age group, any expression or acknowledgment of suicidal thoughts must be taken seriously. If your child makes any comments regarding suicide, including "I just want to die," "I just want this all to end," "Life would be easier if I wasn't around," or any other statements that illustrate risk, an immediate intervention is an absolute necessity. Though you may feel like you are overreacting, you must ask him/her if he/she is feeling suicidal or if he/she has plans to hurt himself/herself. First and foremost, never leave children (or any person for that matter) alone if they have made any type of suicidal remark or gesture. If their level of distress is so severe that they are making suicidal comments, you must do all that you can to keep them safe. Immediate psychiatric help is always available through your local hospital emergency room. Psychiatric staff will be on site to do a thorough suicide assessment and will provide an environment in which your child will be kept safe. If your child's level of distress is so severe that he/she is unwilling to have you intervene by driving him/her to an ER, you can call your local police, who, in most jurisdictions, will send out a psychiatric crisis team or officers who specialize in dealing with individuals who are threatening suicide. This may be frightening for you, but it is critical for interventions to be implemented that provide immediate assessment, access to psychiatric care, and a hospital setting in which your child can be kept safe from self-harm. Keeping your children safe from themselves is paramount.

Just like all other topics discussed in this book, providing a supportive, caring, and loving environment will contribute tremendously toward treatment and recovery from a depressive episode. Actively participating in your child's treatment also includes taking care of yourself. Attending a parenting support group, participating in family therapy, and staying active can help to manage any increase in stress and frustration.

Bipolar disorder (also commonly referred to as manic depression) can also be diagnosed in children and adolescents. Mood instability is a defining characteristic of this disorder and can severely impact your child's psychological and social functioning. An unstable mood can be expressed through both manic and depressive symptoms. Mania in children is often exhibited by marked periods of increased energy; hyperverbal speech (speaking in a rapid manner); sleep problems, including restlessness and the inability to fall asleep; difficulty focusing at home and school; irritability; grandiose thoughts; and engaging in risky or overtly sexual behaviors (http://goo.gl/35nMs). Manic behaviors are usually recognizable because of the dramatic changes that occur within a child's normal range of behavior and emotional expression. One of the main difficulties that treating psychologists, psychiatrists, and other health care professionals have when diagnosing this disorder is that currently no standard in the mental health field characterizes symptoms displayed specifically by children. In a paper published in 2005 discussing treatment options for children with bipolar disorder, Kowatch et al. stated, "The current DSM-IV criteria for mania were developed for adults and are frequently difficult to apply to children. Identifying episode onset and offset can be difficult because many children with BPD (Bipolar Disorder) present with frequent daily mood swings that have been occurring for months to years. Children with BPDs often present with a mixed or dysphoric picture characterized by frequent short periods of intense mood lability and irritability rather than classic euphoric mania" (http://goo.gl/NfA5v). In simple terms, children differ from adults and diagnosis and intervention strategies should be age appropriate and implemented by a mental health professional who understands and works specifically with children and adolescents. Managing mania and depression and the mood deregulation that defines bipolar disorder is challenging, and a multidisciplinary approach can be most beneficial.

If you suspect that your child is beginning to exhibit mood deregulation or an increase in mental health symptoms, a simple but effective tool to track these behaviors is a basic mood/behavior log. This type of tracking system should be kept relatively simple, with the intensity of the exhibited emotion/behavior being described then scored from one (no significant expression) to ten (extreme behavior/volatility that needs immediate psychiatric intervention). The log can also track how long the episode lasted, any known stressors or incidents that may have contributed to the outburst, and the frequency with which it occurred (hourly, daily, or weekly). Documenting sleep patterns or disruptions in the sleep cycle can also provide valuable information. When tracked, this information can be given to a mental health professional, who will then be able to make a more accurate diagnosis and decide on a treatment approach. As the parent of a child suffering from a mental health disorder, it is imperative that you become an expert on the presentation of your child's moods and behaviors. Recognition of any changes in functioning can provide critical information and feedback for the treating mental health professionals.

Attention deficit hyperactivity disorder (ADHD) is one of the more commonly diagnosed mental health disorders in children and adolescents (http://goo.gl/Iq69J). ADHD can be a debilitating illness that causes significant impairment in academic and social functioning. The medications that are used to treat ADHD are classified as psychostimulants. These medications, much like caffeine, for example, accelerate the functioning of the central nervous system. One of the more significant side effects of these medicines, however, is that they can stunt growth.

*Although controversy persists regarding the possible neg-
ative effect of adrenergic stimulants on growth in children with ADHD, the consensus that appears to be
reached in the scientific literature is that stimulant usage may cause a manageable attenuation of growth in
these children...It appears that increased amounts of
dopamine and noradrenaline have the ability to inhibit
the secretion of growth hormone and growth-related
hormones such as prolactin, thyroid hormones, sex hormones, and insulin. Therefore, it would be reason-
able to suggest that the increases in dopamine and
noradrenaline caused by stimulant usage can disrupt
the homeostasis of both growth hormone and growth-
related hormones, generating the potential for the sup-
pression of growth.*(Negrao, 2011)

This is why "medication holidays" are an important adjunct to
any medical treatment for ADHD. A medication holiday is a
predetermined time frame agreed upon by you and your treating physician during which your child will not be administered
medication. Weekends, holidays, and summer break are the
most common times when medication holidays are implemented
in a treatment plan.

The Diagnostic and Statistical Manual lists the following

symptoms as possible indications of ADHD: a person fails to pay close attention to details and is more likely to make careless mistakes; he/she may have difficulty sustaining attention or does not seem to listen when spoken to directly; he/she may exhibit difficulty following through on instructions or organizing tasks and activities. Symptoms also include a reluctance to engage in tasks that require sustained mental effort. Persons with ADHD often lose things necessary for the completion of tasks and are easily distracted and forgetful.

As you read this list, it quickly becomes evident that not only does the DSM describe most children, it describes many adults trying to juggle the vast complexities of life. It is, therefore, important to remember that other criteria must be met. The symptoms have to persist for at least six months and must be considered harmful to the individual. They must also be inconsistent with the developmental level of the person exhibiting the behaviors. The DSM-IV (TR) can provide an even more detailed list for the interested reader.

ADHD is a mental health disorder that clearly relates to brain functioning. This is the main reason that it is so important to differentiate between behavioral problems and ADHD. The interventions for behavioral problems and the treatment for ADHD differ (especially in regard to medication management), and if you are not treating the right disorder, you will not obtain the desired result.

One way to determine whether an individual has ADHD is to use an electroencephalogram (EEG). EEGs are used to measure brain waves. The brain produces different types of waves, but the four most relevant for this discussion are beta, alpha, theta, and delta waves. Beta waves are formed when we are wide awake; alpha waves are produced when we are fatigued or bored; theta waves are produced while we are in the early stages of sleep; and delta waves are formed when we are in REM sleep. If you look at an EEG for an individual with ADHD, you will notice that his brain is producing primarily alpha waves. Let's recall that alpha waves are the tired or bored brain waves. This explains why people with ADHD are so distractible (they're bored) and also why stimulants work to calm them down. The stimulants "speed up" the alpha waves to beta waves that then help them to concentrate.

It is very important for parents to recognize true ADHD and advocate for their children, both when they have ADHD and when symptoms that look like ADHD are actually a manifestation of some other problem. Do not accept at face value any person simply telling you that your child has ADHD. Get him/her tested; have someone do an EEG (a neurologist or health psychologist will be able to either perform the test or provide appropriate referrals). Simply medicating children who do not have ADHD will not work to resolve their behavioral problems. Finally, there are any number of reasons that someone could exhibit psychological symptoms that may indicate or mimic ADHD. Conflict with peers, abuse, trauma, negative pressures at home, and discord between parents can all affect psychological functioning. A full neurological/psychological evaluation is essential in making sure that your child has the right diagnosis (if any) and is getting the appropriate treatment.

To provide the best outcome for a child suffering from any mental health disorder, a multidisciplinary approach must be implemented. For many disorders, psychotropic interventions (psychiatric medications) play a crucial role in the treatment and stabilization of mood symptoms. As an advocate for your child, it is imperative to find a psychiatrist who specializes in the assessment and treatment of children and adolescents. Because of the unique presentation of psychiatric symptoms in children and the possible side effects of treatment, working specifically with a psychiatrist who specializes in children/adolescents will help to address the symptoms that are unique to your child. The primary goal of any psychotropic intervention is for a reduction in mental health symptoms, improved psychosocial functioning (in school, at home, with peers, etc.), and stabilization of any mood disturbances.

Another key component regarding mental health treatment is the importance of medication and treatment compliance. The reality of the situation is that you must become an expert on your child's disorder. Ask questions, advocate, and do not be afraid to educate yourself by studying/reading the most up-to-date and current research regarding treatment options, presentation of negative side effects, and alternative treatment approaches. When helping a child with a mental health disorder, active involvement is crucial. You must help your child to understand and strive for symptom stabilization. Do not hesitate to find support groups for parents with mentally ill children to improve your network of support. These groups are excellent places to learn new intervention strategies, gain insight into treatment options, and manage the stress that comes with raising a mentally ill child.

It is also crucial for the multidisciplinary approach to include individual and family therapy. Again, finding a psychologist who specializes in the treatment of adolescents is vital. His/her approach must be age specific, and he/she needs to have a working knowledge base and expertise in treating the disorder. Do not hesitate to interview a few therapists until you find one who you think would work best with your child. One of the primary goals of treatment is to help your child to gain insight into his mental illness and understand the importance of treatment compliance. Therapy should provide a safe environment in which your child can express his concerns and fears, learn new coping strategies that assist in the management of stress, and emphasize ways to make adaptive decisions regarding all aspects of his life. Family counseling is another option that promotes healthy interaction between all family members. Family therapy is beneficial because it helps to improve communication, decrease stress within the family dynamic, and allow the expression of discontent in a structured and safe environment. In the end, advocacy, understanding, and a willingness to actively participate in your child's treatment will help the long-term prognosis and the management of any mental health disorder.

Mental illness is a complex and challenging issue for any family to deal with. Several concepts discussed in this chapter should be implemented and used as a guide when making decisions regarding mental health treatment. Also provided is a list of references that can be used to help to improve your knowledge base and development of intervention strategies.

1. National Institute of Mental Health: transforming the understanding and treatment of mental illness through re-

search: (`http://goo.gl/mFj2`).

2. Child and Adolescent Bipolar Foundation: (`http://goo.gl/oqwQq`).

3. National Suicide Prevention Lifeline: (`http://goo.gl/rGUS`) 1- 800-273-TALK (8255).

4. Center for Disease Control and Prevention: (`http://goo.gl/kKXe5`).

5. The United States Department of Human Services estimates that at least one in five children and adolescents exhibits enough symptoms to be diagnosed with a mental health disorder, including depression, ADHD, anxiety, conduct, and eating disorders.

6. Psychological disturbances can lead to a significant change in functioning, including poor school performance, family conflict, sexually acting out behaviors, violence, and even suicide.

7. The establishment of a baseline for behavior becomes one of the most important parental assessment techniques. When you have a significant understanding of usual behavior patterns, as well as a context for the behavior, it becomes easier for you to identify potentially worrisome changes.

8. Depressive symptoms in teens often manifest themselves with a significant increase in irritability and agitation. Along with these symptoms, depression in teenagers may also include an increase in sadness and feelings of hopelessness, changes in sleep patterns, difficulty concentrating, loss of appetite, feelings of worthlessness, low self-esteem, and suicidal ideation.

9. When we consider that teenage suicide is the third leading cause of death for fifteen- to twenty-four-year olds, any expression or acknowledgment of suicidal thoughts must be taken seriously. If your child makes any comments regarding suicide, including "I just want to die," "I just want this all to end," "Life would be easier if I wasn't around," or any other statements that illustrate risk, an immediate intervention is an absolute necessity.

10. Mood instability is a defining characteristic of bipolar disorder and can severely impact your child's psychological and social functioning. An unstable mood can be expressed through both manic and depressive symptoms. Mania in children is often exhibited by marked periods of increased energy; hyperverbal speech (speaking in a rapid manner); sleep problems, including restlessness and the inability to fall asleep; difficulty focusing at home and school; irritabil-

ity; grandiose thoughts; and engaging in risky or overtly sexual behaviors (`http://goo.gl/35nMs`).

11. For many disorders, psychotropic interventions (psychiatric medications) play a crucial role in the treatment and stabilization of mood symptoms. As an advocate for your child, it is imperative to find a psychiatrist who specializes in the assessment and treatment of children and adolescents.

12. You must become an expert on your child's disorder. Ask questions, advocate, and do not be afraid to educate yourself by studying/reading the most up-to-date and current research regarding treatment options, presentation of negative side effects, and alternative treatment approaches.

13. It is also crucial for the multidisciplinary approach to include individual and family therapy. Finding a psychologist who specializes in the treatment of adolescents is extremely important. His/her approach must be age specific, and he/she needs to have a working knowledge base and expertise in treating the disorder. Do not hesitate to interview a few therapists until you find one whom you think would work best with your child.

14. Advocacy, understanding, and a willingness to actively participate in your child's treatment will help the long-term

prognosis and the management of any mental health disorder.

About the Authors

Aaron Cannon PhD. has been practicing clinical psychology with an emphasis on wellness, family dynamics and health for the past 14 years. He has made several media appearances most notably on talk radio and conducts workshops on effective parenting. Dr. Cannon has provided individual, family and couples counseling in a variety of therapeutic settings. He has extensive training in Psychological Assessment, individual and family therapy, and crisis intervention. He has been married for 14 years and has two children.

Albert Oppedisano, Psy.D has worked as a clinical and forensic psychologist for the past thirteen years. He is a hostage negotiator who has taught extensively at the California Department of Corrections Hostage Negotiator Academy focusing on the development of active listening and effective communication. Dr. Oppedisano provides marriage, family and child counseling to police agencies, city personnel and their families. Additionally, he provides 24-hour Critical Incident Intervention Debriefings for Officer Involved Shootings, Line of Duty Deaths, and other traumatic incidents. He has been married for twelve years and has one child.

Dr. Oppedisano and Dr. Cannon are available for speaking engagements and seminars. Please visit 21stcenturypsychology.com for more information, blog posts and a variety of other resources.

Bibliography

[1] (n.d.). Retrieved from http://www.purematters.com/healthy-body/ sexual-health/sex-talk-taking-place-after-the-fact.

[2] (n.d.). Retrieved from http://www.cdc.gov/hiv/default.htm.

[3] (n.d.). Retrieved from http://pubs.niaaa.nih.gov/publications/arh284/205212.htm.

[4] (n.d.). Retrieved from http://odp.idaho.gov/Underage_Drinking_Tabloid.pdf.

[5] (n.d.). Retrieved from http://www.nimh.nih.gov/science-news/2010/national-survey-confirms -that-youth-are-disproportionately-affected-by-mental-disorders.shtml.

[6] (n.d.). Retrieved from http://mentalhealth.samhsa.gov/publications/allpubs/CA0004/default.asp.

[7] (n.d.). Retrieved from http://www.bpkids.org/learn/library/about-pediatric-bipolar-disorder.

[8] (n.d.). Retrieved from http://www.csom.org/train/etiology/4/4_1.htm.

[9] (n.d.). Retrieved from http://bjs.ojp.usdoj.gov/index.cfm.

[10] (n.d.). Retrieved from http://www.wsipp.wa.gov/rptfiles/Soff_recid.pdf.

[11] (n.d.). Retrieved from http://www.bpchildren.org/files/Download/TreatmentGuidelines.pdf.

[12] (n.d.). Retrieved from http://www.cdc.gov/ncbddd/adhd/data.html.

[13] (n.d.). Retrieved from http://www.cdc.gov/ViolencePrevention/pdf/Electronic _Aggression_Researcher_Brief-a.pdf.

[14] Aria, A. K. 2008. High School Drinking Mediates the Relationship Between Parental Monitoring and College Drinking: A Longitudinal Analysis. Substance Abuse Treatment, Prevention & Policy, 11-31.

[15] American Psychiatric Association. 2000) Diagnostic and Statistical Manual of Mental Disorders (revised 4th ed.). Washington, DC:

[16] Banks, J. 2002. Childhood Discipline: Challenges for Clinicians and Parents. American Family Physician, 1447-1453.

[17] Caputo, R. K. 2005. Religiousness and Adolescent Behaviors: A Comparison of Boys and Girls. Journal of Religion and Spirituality in Social Work, 39-67.

[18] Crafts, W. F., M. Lietsch, and M. Lietsch. 1909. Intoxicating Drinks and Drugs. New York City: International Reform Bureau.

[19] Haynie, D.L., K. H. Beck, A. D. Crump, D. Shattuck, and B. Simons-Morton. 1999. Parenting Strategies Regarding Teen Behavior: Parent and Teen Perceptions. American Journal of Health Behavior, 403-414.

[20] Forhan, S. E., S. L. Gottlieb, M. Sternberg, F. Xu, S. D. Datta, G. M. McQuillan, et al. 2009. Prevalence of Sexually Trasmitted Infections Among Female Adolescents Aged 14 to 19 in the United States. Pediatrics, 1505-1512.

[21] Haynie, D. B.-M. 1999. Parenting Strategies Regarding Teen Behavior: Parent and Teen Perceptions. American Journal of Health Behavior, 403-414.

[22] Lindesmith, A. R. 1968. Addiction and Opiates. Chicago: Aldine Publishing.

[23] Mahima, S. P. 2008. Relationship between Parental Overindulgence and Buying Behavior in the Context of Invasive Marketing: A Comparative Study of Two Cultures. Seoul Journal of Business, 31-53.

[24] Nash, S. M. 2005. Pathways to Adolescent Alcohol Use: Family Environment, Peer Influence, and Parental Expectations. The Journal of Adolescent Health, 19-28.

[25] Negrao, B. V. 2011. Stimulants and Growth in Children with Attention-Deficit/Hyperactivity Disorder. Medical Hypotheses, 21-28.

[26] Romaine, P. 2009. Positive Parenting: Building Character in Young People. New York: Do It Now Foundation.

[27] Tapert, S. C. 2004. Alcohol and the Adolescent Brain: Human Studies. Alcohol Research and Health, 205-212.

[28] Watkins, K. E. 2006. An Update on Adolescent Drug Use: What School Counselors Need to Know. Journal of Professional School Counseling, 131-138.

[29] White, A. 2003. Substance Use and Adolescent Brain Development. Youth Studies Australia, 39.

[30] Woodside, M. 1988. Research on Children of Alcoholics: Past and Future. British Journal of Addiction, 785-792.

Made in the USA
Charleston, SC
20 October 2013